To Have and To Hold

Richard Bean

T0284308

methuen | drama

LONDON • NEW YORK • OXFORD • NEW DELHI • SYDNEY

METHUEN DRAMA
Bloomsbury Publishing Plc
50 Bedford Square, London, WC1B 3DP, UK
1385 Broadway, New York, NY 10018, USA
29 Earlsfort Terrace, Dublin 2, Ireland

BLOOMSBURY, METHUEN DRAMA and the Methuen
Drama logo are trademarks of Bloomsbury Publishing Plc

First published in Great Britain 2023

A catalogue record for this book is available from the British Library.

A catalog record for this book is available from the Library of Congress.

ISBN: PB: 978-1-3504-4854-4
ePDF: 978-1-3504-4856-8
eBook: 978-1-3504-4855-1

Series: Modern Plays

Typeset by Mark Heslington Ltd, Scarborough, North Yorkshire

To find out more about our authors and books visit
www.bloomsbury.com and sign up for our newsletters.

To Have and To Hold was first presented at Hampstead Theatre on 26 October 2023, with the following cast and creative team:

Jack	**Alun Armstrong**
Florence	**Marion Bailey**
Pamela	**Rachel Dale**
Tina	**Hermione Gulliford**
Rob	**Christopher Fulford**
Eddie	**Adrian Hood**

Writer	Richard Bean
Co-Directors	Richard Wilson and Terry Johnson
Designer	James Cotterill
Lighting	Bethany Gupwell
Sound	John Leonard
Casting	Robert Sterne CDG

Note from the author

My father was apprenticed at fourteen as a blacksmith and then joined the Hull police, serving the people of Hull for twenty years. He loved to tell his stories, and the 'stories' in this play are his but he is not Jack Kirk, and Florence is not my mother. My parents have never been the victims of the theft that is a plot point in the play. The Kirks, and the other characters in the play, are inventions. I wished that my father had recorded his many stories in some form, and this play, if it achieves anything, does that for four of them.

I dedicate this play to my brilliant parents and my loving family.

To Have and To Hold

Cast in order of appearance

Florence Kirk, *90*
Robert (Rob) Kirk, *60*
Pamela Granger, *55*
Jack Kirk, *91*
Tina Keenan (née Kirk), *58*
Eddie, *55*

Set

*A three bedroomed semi-detached house in the village of Wetwang,
East Yorkshire. It is away from the main road on a quiet cul-de-sac.
The house was built in the 1960s. Back stage, running up from up
stage right to up stage left, is a flight of stairs with a stair lift. The
stairs run into a hall and reception room, off which, through sliding
double doors, is a dining room with a serving hatch to the kitchen.
The back garden can be accessed through French windows at the end
of the dining room. Stage right is the front door, to a drive and the
front garden. The décor is to suit the generation born around 1930,
with a love of flowers, and the countryside. Paintings depict rural
and moorland scenes, but a few also show policemen in comic
scenarios, asleep on the beat, on scooters etc. There are two
photographs mounted on the wall above the cupboard under the
stairs – one is of* **Rob** *on his graduation day; one is of* **Tina** *on her
graduation day. A collection of random photographs of
grandchildren dominates the wall below the graduation photographs
as a kind of grand mosaic of the legacy of life they will leave. Before
the door is a low table, the siting of a landline telephone. Centre
stage is a three seater sofa. Down stage right is an armchair with a
hydraulic foot support. Down stage left is* **Jack**'s *chair, again it has a
hydraulic foot support function. Next to it is a wooden lockable
cabinet on top of which is set an old cassette recorder/player and some
loose home recorded tapes of Jim Reeves. By* **Jack**'s *chair on a low
side table are set spectacles on a carved nose stand, a magnifying
glass, nail clippers, tissues, TV remote, the* Daily Mail, *a coaster for
tea cups and a second handset for the landline phone. Down stage
right is a television in a cabinet with a Freeview box.*

Rob   Tina said she was worried about you.

Florence   Nowt. Bit of water works.

Rob   But you're OK now?

Florence   Yes. The smell in here's your dad.

Rob *starts looking in his briefcase and comes up with a mobile phone charger which he plugs into the wall and connects his phone.*

Florence   What do you think you're doing?

He does the same with his laptop.

Rob   Charging my phone.

Florence   And what's that?

Rob   My laptop. Could I charge my phone and laptop please, Mum?

Florence   Bloke came to acid clean the oven and fost thing he done was plug his phone in the wall. Your dad made the lad give him a pound.

Rob   I don't believe you. Dad's no interest in money.

Florence   It's the principle. Fish pie tonight.

Rob (*ironically*)   Smashing.

Florence   Tea or coffee? The coffee's out of a jar.

Rob   Tea then.

Florence   We don't pay four quid for a cup of coffee round here. We're not that daft.

Rob   Tea's fine, Mum. Drop of red top.

Florence   We don't have red milk. I'll not pay good money for water to nobody. Especially Germans.

Rob   Germans?

Florence   Lidl!

She goes off into the kitchen and converses through the serving hatch.

Florence (*off*)   You eat rubbish, but our coffee's not good enough. Me and your dad, we've lived this long 'cause all we eat is fresh.

(*Through the hatch.*) Will you take us to Lidl tomorrow?

Rob   Of course. How's his mood?

Florence   He's like the grand old Duke of York.

Rob   Is he half way up or half way down?

Florence   Talking about going to Switzerland, to where you pay 'em to kill you.

Rob   Dignitas? Was that your idea?

Florence   Stop it!

Rob   You talk him out of it, do you?

Florence   No! I say, 'Go! It'd do you good. Broaden your horizons. You've never been abroad.'

Rob   Tina said he's stopped driving.

Florence   I don't care, I've stopped gerrin in. I've been through enough hedges at fifty mile an hour for a lifetime.

Rob   How do you get to the bank?

Florence   Bank's closed. Pamela does a little shop for us every now and then.

Rob   Oh no.

We hear the electric kettle beginning to heat. Enter **Florence**.

Rob   Where's the fish from?

Florence   The Arctic I should think.

Rob   Very funny.

Florence   Rhubarb Eddie. He gives us one every week.

Rob   Haddock Eddie surely?

Florence   Ask him yourself, he's coming to do the lawn.

Rob   Rhubarb Eddie. I know Yorkshire. I bet thirty years ago he tried to force a stem of rhubarb in a bucket and it died. Folks enjoyed his failure so much they coined the appellation Rhubarb Eddie.

Florence   I'm glad I never went to university.

Florence *retreats into the kitchen. The doorbell rings.* **Florence** *re-enters.*

Rob   I'll go, Mum!

Rob *stands and goes to the door.* **Rob** *tries the door. It's locked.*

Rob   It's locked.

Jack (*off*)   Who's that?

Florence   How the hell do I know?!

Florence *unlocks the door but doesn't open it.*

Jack (*off*)   Find out then!

Florence (*off*)   I'm not wasting my time finding out, they're gonna come in in a minute and then it'll be obvious!

Rob *opens the door.*

Rob   Pam! Hi!

Pamela   Rob! Fancy seeing you here!

Pamela *enters. She is a woman of about 55 and wearing the livery and protective clothing of a franchised veterinary chain. She carries a two litre plastic bottle of blue top milk and a Tesco carrier bag with vegetables. They don't kiss or shake hands.*

Rob   It's Pamela!

Jack (*off*)   What does she want? She's always round here!

Rob   Are you?

Florence   Hello, luv.

Pamela   Hi, Flo.

Florence   She's brought your milk!

(*To* **Pamela**.) When did you last see Tina, him, Robert.

Rob   The funeral of the old racist.

Pamela   Uncle Arthur.

Florence   Racist? He was always nice to me.

Pamela   How's Uncle Jack today?

Florence   Coughing up a lot of muck.

Rob   Who's his GP? I'll take him.

Florence   A GP appointment?! Next Sheffield flood.

Rob   GPs, that's Tina's bailiwick.

Pamela   You and your words. I brought you some veg, Flo.

Florence   Do you want a tea, love?

Pamela   Please. Haven't seen cousin Rob for –

Florence (*shouting*)   – do you want tea up there?!

Jack (*off*)   Don't be stupid, I've just had one!

Florence *exits too the kitchen.*

Pamela   Your mam's struggling.

Rob   Yeah?

Pamela   It was alright when your dad could drive, 'cause they could get to Lidl and do the shop together.

Rob   I'm taking her to Lidl tomorrow. How do they get cash?

Pamela   They give their card to Eddic.

Rob   Oh no. What's he like?

Pamela   Typical pig man.

Rob   Can he be trusted?

Pamela   I wouldn't give him my bank card.

Rob   Jesus.

Pamela   What will you do with Jack's car?

Rob   Sell it I guess.

Pamela   Your mum's lonely. And depressed. Everyone they knew in the village has died. It's no trouble for me, here's not much of a detour from the vet's, you know, to drop the milk off.

Rob   What do we owe you?

Pamela   It's not about money, Rob.

Rob   OK, OK, I'm here now. How's your mother?

Pamela   She's had her hip done, but she's not been able to drive, not been able to come out here and see your mum.

Rob   I wished they'd move back to Hull. Suit my mother to be able to pop in on your mum. Sisters.

Pamela   He's given up, your dad. I took them out, me and Alan –

Rob   – your husband?

Pamela   We've split up, amicably. Alan likes your dad's police stories. We took them both out for your dad's birthday. You were in LA.

Rob   I rang him. Five o'clock in the morning, my time.

Pamela   Well done. In the pub after the meal he just put his head on the table, his forehead. It was like he couldn't bear it.

Rob   I should've been there.

Pamela   This isn't criticism.

Rob   No, sure.

Pamela   We're all proud of you. I've read all the novels.

Rob   Have you?

Pamela   The Inspector Jenus ones.

Rob   Jenus? (*Pronounced Jeenus.*)

Pamela   Is he you?

Rob   Er . . . no. I don't smoke, I'm not a sex addict, I've never had a gambling problem, or a parrot –

Pamela   – no but –

Rob   – I don't live in Cambridge on a canal boat with a 22-year-old Thai bride. Why do you think he's me?

Pamela   Because everything he says sounds like you.

Rob   I give in. He's me.

Enter **Florence**, *struggling with two cups on a tray, with two pieces of iced cherry cake. They both stand up instinctively to help but it's* **Pamela** *who takes the tray off her.*

Florence   Them's real them cherries. Eat 'em, they're not for show.

Rob   Thanks, Mum.

Florence   I heard you talking about me.

Pamela   No, no.

Rob   Pam says you're lonely.

Florence   I never see nobody stuck out here. I don't know nobody in Wetwang.

Rob   You could've gone to Tina's for Christmas.

Florence   Your dad won't travel. Needs a pee every half hour. They can invent a car that drives itself, but where's the car with a urinal? Can you mash the mash for me, Tina, Robert.

Rob   Of course.

Florence *heads back to the kitchen.*

Pamela   She doesn't have the strength.

Rob   For mashing?

Pamela   Do you get to see Suki?

Rob   She comes to me in London. I have to go and get her obviously.

Pamela   Tina's done well hasn't she. Private GPs isn't it?

Rob   Yes, she has no shame. She's driving up today.

Pamela   So you're both going to be here?

Rob   Why, is that a problem?

Pamela   Your mum and dad sleep in separate rooms now.

Rob   I know they do. They're my parents.

Pamela   I didn't mean –

Rob   – no, you didn't. I'm sleeping on the sofa.

Pamela   You seem annoyed by me being –

Rob   – no! It's really good of you to pop in on them.

Pamela   I work local.

Rob   Pam, I appreciate everything that I didn't know you were doing.

Pamela   They don't need the two of you here, just someone –

Rob   – Dad asked both of us to come up.

Pamela   An announcement?

Rob   Maybe he's willing to move.

Pamela   A move would kill him. He's waiting for God.

Rob   Thanks for the milk.

Pamela   I hope you don't think that I'm judging you. But they need you now.

She stands, picks up her cake and goes into the kitchen.

(*Off.*) I'll see you, Flo. I'll take the cake with me. You don't need shopping then?

Florence (*off*)   Rob's taking me to Lidl tomorrow.

Pamela (*off*)   I know, you'll enjoy that.

Enter **Pamela** *from kitchen.*

Rob   Bye, Pam. Thanks.

Pamela   Let me know about the car.

Rob   You're interested in buying the car?

Pamela   Depends what he's doing with it. Bye. I hope you haven't –

Rob   – no! I've not taken anything the wrong way.

She has opened the door and is half through it.

Pamela   It's just that, you know, you can't wipe his bum by Skype.

Rob   I'm sure they're working on it.

Pamela *exits.*

Rob (*to himself*)   Jeez! She always was horrible.

Florence *comes back into the living room.*

Florence (*whispering*)   I caught your dad, yesterday, Friday, watching a blue movie.

Rob   Porn?

Florence   Yes, after tea, about nine. This lass, just stood there, not a stitch on

Rob   Oh no.

Florence   The camera right up on, her you know, . . . chuff
. . . and she had that tattooed and pierced nipples an' all.

Rob   And Dad was . . . what?

Florence   He heard me gasp and then he switched it off.
Eddie brings him stuff in jiffy bags.

Rob   But you don't have a video player. Let's see what
you've got.

Rob *turns the TV on and checks out the channels with the remote.
He mutes the sound. All they have is a standard set top box, not Sky
or BT.*

Florence   We bicker but I like him. But if he's watching
blue movies, I don't want to live with him. He'll have that in
his head.

Rob   This is Freeview, you don't have any porn channels at
all, oh wait a minute. Babestation. That's presumably babes.
But it's not on until after midnight.

Florence   This was about nine o'clock.

Rob   I can set the parental controls.

Florence   What does that mean?

Rob   Normally it's a password set by the parents to stop the
children watching. But if I do it now, it's a password set by
the children to stop the parents watching.

*He sets the parental controls. A beep is heard. It's the stair lift. The
stair lift is moving.* **Jack** *appears sat on it, holding a walking stick
and hugging a clear bag full of used tissues. He is wearing pyjamas
and a heavy dressing gown. He looks weak and dreadful. He coughs
as he comes down.* **Rob** *stands, as if to help him off the chair of the
chair lift.*

Florence   Robert's here.

Jack   I can see that and I know his name, I an't gorr
Alzheimer's.

Florence   I an't gorr Alzheimer's!

Jack   I never said you did have, I said, I an't gorr Alzheimer's.

He gets off the chair lift and using a stick gets to his armchair and sits down with a groan. He sits in his armchair and operates the leg support violently. His legs fly up.

Like a bloody moon shot.

He starts coughing.

Florence   The exercise has set him off.

Jack   You've set me off!

He is coughing.

Get me some kitchen roll, son.

Florence   No. That's my kitchen roll, for my kitchen, and no spitting, not in my living room, we've got guests.

Jack   He's not a guest, he's our son.

Florence   If you want to spit, go in the loo.

Jack   I've just sat down!

Rob *finds a box of tissues which he gives to* **Jack**.

Rob   I'd like you to spit, so I can see what colour it is.

Jack *doesn't spit, more of a wipe. He looks at the sputum.* **Rob** *stands and looks at the tissue which is held open by* **Jack**.

Rob   Red specks.

Jack   I'm ninety bloody one! There's red specks in everything. I'm not gonna hospital! Ever again. Never!

Rob   Bit final.

Jack   Aye, everything's final. We're in the finals.

Florence   What colour is it?

Jack   If you go in the garage there's a Dulux colour chart.

Jack *folds the tissue and disposes of it in a bin for the purpose beside his chair.*

Rob   I'll take you to the hospital for an X-ray.

Jack   That's where I caught this. There was nowt wrong with me.

Rob   What were you in for?

Jack   Pacemaker MOT. I've got to go back in a month.

Jack *gives* **Rob** *a letter.*

Rob   Where is it?

Florence   In his chest.

Jack   Which hospital?!

Florence   It'll be Infirmary.

Jack   It's Castle Hill! Don't listen to her. She can't see.

Florence   I can see!

Jack   Only with them eyes in the back of your head!

Florence   Pam's fancy man's taking him to that one.

Rob   Ooh! Pam has a new fellah? Fast worker.

Florence   Lives York way. Pointy shoes. You can always judge a man by his shoes.

Jack   Rubbish!

Florence   I was right about Gary Glitter!

Rob   I'll take you, Dad.

Jack   I'm not going.

Florence   You've perked him up Robert. He 'ant coughed for five minutes.

Jack *starts coughing.*

Florence   You did that deliberately! And don't spit!

The phone rings.

Jack   Oh bloody hell!

Florence   Who's that now?

Jack *picks his phone up.* **Florence** *picks the hall phone up.*

Jack   Am I getting it?!

(*Into phone.*) Hello?

Florence (*into phone*)   Hello.

Have you got it?

Jack   You're getting it, are you?

They put the phones down simultaneously.

Why have you put the phone down?

Florence   I thought you had it!

Jack   I did have it, and then you got involved!

Florence   You said hello!

Jack   I say hello to everyone!

Florence   Why did you put the phone down?!

Jack   I thought you had it!

Florence   I did have it!

Jack   Why did you put it down then?!

Florence   I thought you had it!

Jack   I bloody did have it!

Florence   Who was it then?!

Jack   How the bloody hell do I know? I put it down.

Rob   Let's call them.

(*Picking up the phone.*) One-four-seven-one.

Jack   Who's he ringing now?

Rob   It was a mobile phone number.

Jack   Who is it?!

Rob (*on phone*)   Hello, you just rang?

(*To the room.*) It's Tina.

Florence   Tina? Who's Tina?

Rob   Your daughter.

Florence   Oh our Tina.

Jack   Shouldn't be on her phone, driving.

Rob (*to* **Jack**)   She says she's fifty-eight, she'll drive how she likes.

(*To* **Florence**.) She's in Lidl.

Florence   We're Lidling in the morning.

Rob (*on the phone*)   Lidling, a verb. To buy cheap stuff you don't need, as in 'Yesterday I Lidled a mobile pizza oven'.

Florence   Eggs!

Rob (*on the phone*)   Eggs.

Jack   We've got eggs.

Florence   I've had 'em all.

Jack   When did you have eggs?

Florence   Dinner. An omelette.

Jack   You had a secret omelette?

Florence   There was nowt secret about it.

Jack   You had a boiled egg for breakfast.

Florence   Did I?

Jack   You'll be egg bound now. Get one of them Movicols down your neck sharpish!

(*To* **Rob**.) Your mother forgets things.

Florence   I forget why I married you.

Rob (*on phone*)   A dozen eggs.

Florence   Fifteen! Germans do eggs in fifteens.

Rob (*on phone*)   See you in a bit.

He puts the phone down.

Jack   We get on like a housing estate on fire when no-one else is here. Don't we, love?

Florence   No, we don't.

Jack   Now, let's talk about this charging business.

He pokes at the charging equipment as if it was a dead rat.

We had a bloke come to clean the oven –

Florence   – he's had that story.

Rob   Not believable.

Florence   How come?

Rob   Yorkshire folk spending money on professional oven cleaning.

Jack   It was your mother's wedding anniversary.

Rob   Romantic.

Florence   It was my idea.

Jack   She didn't want owt fancy, she wanted her oven cleaned and I wanted to see what an acid bath looked like.

Florence   The lad has an acid bath in the back of his van.

Jack   Tidgy. Not big enough for what I need it for.

He winks at **Rob**.

Rob   When we're in Driffield tomorrow I can get some cash out the wall for you. Which bank closed?

Florence   NatWest.

Jack   They wrote to us saying they wanted us to –

Florence   – get lost.

Jack   Go paperless.

Florence   Which means 'get lost'.

Jack   They want us on the internet.

Rob   You don't have the internet.

Florence   He won't have it in the house.

Rob   The bank have to give you paper statements if you ask.

Florence   He tried ringing for statements.

Jack   He? Who's he? The cat's basket?

Florence   He'd couldn't remember his mother's maiden name.

Jack   Simpson!

Florence   Like Wallis Simpson. She ran off with the King.

Jack   My mother did not run off with the King.

Florence   He couldn't prove to the bank that he is who he thinks he is.

Jack   I know who I am!

Florence   I was there, you had no idea who you were!

Rob   Pam told me you give Rhubarb Eddie your card and he goes to an ATM somewhere.

Jack   Aye.

Rob   He might be withdrawing a hundred and only giving you fifty.

Jack   He gives me the ticket.

Rob   He withdraws fifty for you, gets a receipt, and then he does a second transaction for another fifty, and doesn't get a ticket.

Florence   Oh no, he's such a nice lad.

Rob   Lad? How old is he?

Florence   Fifty-five.

Jack   I can spot a bad 'un. And, we've got loads of money. Police pension, a state pension, twenty thousand in premium bonds, we're bloody loaded!

Florence   He never thinks about money.

Jack   You can't take it with you!

Rob   Am I still getting the allotment because –?

Florence   – no, Eddie's got that.

Rob   He's doing well, isn't he. He's got my allotment and your bank card. What do you do when you need to set up a direct debit?

Florence   Pamela brings her little computer.

Rob   But there's no internet.

Jack   She puts it next to her phone.

Florence   And then it works.

Rob   So you do have internet banking. Does Pamela print out statements?

Florence   It's all on the screen.

Jack   Talking of Eddies. Do you remember Eddie Arnold? CID, lived off Sutton Park.

Rob   The chip shop siege? Got shot in the willy with an air pistol?

Jack   That's him.

Rob   What about him?

Florence   He's dead.

Jack   Who's telling this story? Me or you?

Rob   I'd like to get down all your police stories.

Jack   Get down? What does that mean?

Rob   This phone has a voice record function.

Florence   He won't have that.

Jack   For you, to use, for your Inspector Jenus?

Rob   No, no, no. For everyone. They're your life. Mum, can you persuade him.

Florence   Me? Persuade him? An't you been watching?

She stands and goes over to **Jack**.

Florence   Gimme that cup.

Jack   Get out of my light!

Florence *grabs the cup and leaves to the kitchen with it.*

Rob   It would be a kind of immortality.

A car pulls up outside.

Jack   Someone in the drive. I've had enough of this life, never mind living forever.

Rob   The stories would be a gift, for my Suki, and Tina's kids.

The doorbell chimes.

Florence (*off*)   Who's that?!

Rob   I'll go, Mum!

Rob *opens the door.* **Eddie** *is there, holding an armful of rhubarb. He stands outside on the step in his wellies. He is a farm labourer type of about 50.*

Eddie (*off*)   How do? Brought this for Mrs Kirk.

Rob   Come in.

Eddie *gives* **Rob** *the rhubarb.*

Eddie (*off*)   I'll take these off fost.

Rob *leaves the door open and heads towards the kitchen with the mass of rhubarb but is met by* **Florence**.

Florence   Who have you left out there?

Rob   My guess would be 'Rhubarb Eddie'.

Enter **Eddie** *in socks.*

Florence   It is! (*To* **Rob**.) How did you know it was him?

Eddie   How do, Flo?

Florence   Alright, Eddie luv, thank you. I'd complain if I thought anyone cared, but they don't, so I just get on with it.

Florence *locks the door behind him and puts the key in her pocket.*

Eddie   How do, Jack?

Jack   What you got there, Eddie?

Eddie   Rhubarb.

Jack   I'm sick of the bloody stuff.

Florence   I'm not, I love rhubarb. Give it here.

She takes the rhubarb off of **Rob**.

Florence   This is my son Tina, Robert.

Eddie   So that's what a novelist looks like, eh?

Florence   Sit down, love, or are you in a rush?

Jack   He'll be here all day now.

Eddie   I'll take the weight of mi plates.

Florence   Plates! Ha, ha.

(*To* **Rob**.) That's his feet.

Rob   Cockney rhyming, plates of meat, feet.

Eddie *sits in the armchair downstage right and operates the violent foot support.*

Eddie   Wahey!

Florence   You love that, don't you!

Eddie *plays with the controls, does the violent lift a second time.*

Eddie   Giovanni, at the skip, he's looking out for one these for us.

Jack   You'll bust it. Daft lummox.

Florence   Are you gonna mow the lawn today, Eddie luv?

Eddie   I thought I'd sit here and do nowt and in an hour's time you give us fifty quid to bugger off.

Florence   He's a card, in't he! Mows the lawn in his bare feet like whatshername.

Jack   Oh no! Here we go!

Rob   Like who, Mum?

Florence   That famous woman –

Jack   – Mary Magdalene! Joan of Arc! Boudica!

Eddie   Myra Hindley. Twiggy.

Jack   Raquel Welch. Greta Thunderbird.

Florence   Singer!

Jack   Patsy Cline.

Eddie   Dolly Parton. Susan Boyle.

Jack   Kathy Kirby. Cilla Black.

Florence   Summat to do with the seaside.

Jack   Sandy Shaw!

Florence   That's her.

Jack   Sandy Shaw didn't mow her lawn in her bare feet!

Florence   Did you ever see her with shoes on?

Jack   No.

Florence   Shut up then.

Jack   Eddie, when you do the lawn today, can you pull up the forget-me-nots and trample grass cuttings all over the kitchen floor?

Eddie   Why would you want me to do that?

Jack   'Cause that's what you did last time.

Florence *laughs,* **Eddie** *laughs.*

Eddie   Got your spondoolies here.

Jack   An 'undred.

Eddie *takes out a wallet and finds the notes which he gives to* **Jack**.

Rob   So, you go to Driffield and get cash out for Mum and Dad?

Eddie   Aye. Hole in the wall at the Midland.

Jack   Receipt!

Eddie *leafs through the receipts in his wallet.* **Florence** *laughs through his act.*

Eddic   Curry; curry; curry; Chinese; Alka Seltzer.

Florence   Curry curry curry Chinese Alka Seltzer!

Jack   You've done that joke before.

Eddie   Midland Bank!

Eddie *hands over the receipt to* **Jack**.

Jack   Where's my card?

Florence   That's not your card, it's mine.

Jack   It's a joint account!

Florence   Yes, and we've got two cards, and that one's mine.

Eddie *produces the card and moves to give it to* **Florence**.

Jack   Keep it, 'cause I need you to get another hundred out for petrol for him and his sister.

Rob   I don't need petrol money, Dad.

Florence   You're getting it, you're all treated the same.

Eddie   I'm in Driffield tomorrow.

Florence   Where have you been working this week, luv?

Eddie   I had a couple of days shearing at Watton, Manor Farm.

Rob   Sheep shearing?

Eddie   No, pigs.

Florence   Ha, ha! You can't shear pigs!

Florence *gets a hanky out, knowing she's going to be laughing.* **Eddie***'s pleased.*

Rob   Why do they call you Rhubarb Eddie?

Eddie   'Cause mi fost name's Edward.

Florence   Ha, ha! It's the rhubarb he wants explaining!

Eddie   I have three allotments, dedicated to rhubarb. Easy to grow once you know how

Rob   What's the secret with rhubarb?

Eddie   Hoss shit.

Florence   Ha, ha! Hoss shit!

Rob   Do you force it?

Eddie   I have nowt to do with the hoss.

Florence *laughs almost uncontrollably.* **Jack** *is laughing too.*

Jack   You'll kill her one day, being this hilarious.

Florence   You'll have a tea won't you, Eddie?

Eddie   Aye. Yorkshire, please. Leave the bag in.

Florence *leaves.*

Rob   How do you manage to get three allotments?

Eddie   There's your dad's, another fellah dropped dead and no one told the council, and I've had mi own dad's forever.

Jack   You can do what you like with mine, it's over for me.

Eddie (*sings*)   It's over!

Florence (*through the serving hatch*)   Are we getting a song today?

Eddie   Roy Orbison. 1964. Two weeks at number one.

Florence (*serving hatch*)   He likes his pub quiz does Eddie!

Jack   Shut that hatch! It's like living in a bloody cuckoo clock!

Eddie   Am I getting a story today, Jack, or am I straight out there on the lawn?

Rob   Oh, you normally get a story, do you?

Eddie   Police story, aye. The Cornish pasties, that's my favourite.

Rob   Happens to be my favourite too.

Eddie   The queer tug boat captain? Tragic, obviously, but I did piss mesen.

Florence (*serving hatch opens*)   You can't say 'queer' no more, Eddie.

Jack   What's he said that he can't say?

Florence (*serving hatch*)   Talking about your puff tug boat skipper.

Rob   'Queer' is nowadays a legitimate academic perspective, and is acceptable in modern cultural discourse. Puff, mother . . . isn't.

Florence (*serving hatch*)   The mash is ready for mashing.

Rob   Coming.

Jack   The coal man?

Rob   That's a good one.

Eddie   Not heard it.

Rob *exits to the kitchen, the kitchen door closes.* **Eddie** *passes over the jiffy bag.* **Jack** *secretes it under his chair.*

Eddie   Here you go, Jack. Quick.

Jack   Have I paid you?

Eddie   You did, yeah.

He sits back down.

What's behind this one? Sex or money?

Jack   Sex. Nineteen fifty-eight, Mrs Fletcher says her husband's gone out with the coal lorry but hasn't come back. He'd been in a mood with the daughter who'd been seeing Mickey Richards, Hull's devil incarnate. The daughter shared a flat on Boulevard. Her flat mate said that the night before she'd gone to see Mickey at this empty house on Newbridge Street. I asked why they was meeting at an empty house. Sex was the answer and I nodded innocently, as if it had never crossed my mind. Upstairs at Newbridge Street, blood all over the walls but no body so the coal man had caught them in flagrante delicto –

Eddie   – eh?

Jack On the job . . . he started a fight and lost. I had the *Hull Daily Mail* publicise the story. The coal lorry was found out at Sunk Island, ten miles down the Humber. It was parked just over the bridge of a dyke that fed the Humber. A body dumped there would end up in the sea.

Eddie He'll have put the body in a coal bag.

Jack That's what I'd do. Mickey's mother lived in Sutton and worked as a cleaner in the church hall. She didn't know where Mickey was, naturally. He'd worked as a grave digger and the vicar showed me which of the double decker tombs you could hide in. One had a smell of urine and an empty bottle of stout. The local butcher told me that that day, Mickey's mother had bought half a pound of lamb's liver and two pork chops.

Eddie She's hiding him.

Jack That night I hid up in the belfry which give us a view all across Sutton. At about eleven Mickey's mam left her house carrying a cloth bag. She let hersen in the Church Hall, and ten minutes later, she went home, no bag. I raised the vicar for the key and searched the Church Hall. There was a white wooden chair set in the middle of a storeroom. Looking up, there was a hatch into the roof space. Standing on the same chair I pushed the hatch up and shone my torch straight into Mickey's face. The cheeky bugger said 'Have you found the body?' I said 'No'. He said 'Smashing, I'll be alright then' and he came down as cocky as you like.

Eddie Did he get off?

Jack Aye! No body. He wouldn't get away with it today, not with all the forensics. Catching 'em is only half the game.

Eddie You godda be desperate to spend a night in a tomb.

He stands.

Lawn!

He leaves through the dining room French windows.

(*Off.*) Two pork chops, ha ha!

Jack   People make stupid mistakes!

He opens the locked cabinet and puts the jiffy bag inside and locks it again. The doorbell rings. Followed by an attempt to open a locked door.

Can you hear that!

The doorbell rings again. **Florence** *opens the serving hatch.*

Florence   Is that you doing that?

Jack   How can I ring the doorbell when I'm sat here inside?

Tina (*off*)   The door's locked.

Enter **Rob**. *He tries the door. He finds that it is locked.*

Rob   It's locked.

Florence   What have you done with the key?

Enter **Florence**. *The doorbell rings again.*

Jack   You locked the door after Eddie come in.

Florence   So where's the key?

Jack   What do you normally do with it?

Florence   I put it in my pocket.

Jack   Look in your bloody pocket then.

She does, and finds it.

Florence   Found it!

Jack   I told you it was in there.

Florence   I found it.

Jack   Take the glory, go on! I've gorr enough medals.

The doorbell rings again.

Give it a rest?!

Rob   It's Tina.

Jack   She's got a bloody key!

Florence *unlocks and opens the door.* **Tina** *comes in carrying a Lidl shopping bag and a wine carrier with a selection of bottles and a huge bunch of rhubarb. She hugs her mother.*

Tina   Hi, Mum.

Florence   Hello, luv.

Tina   I picked up some lovely rhubarb.

Jack   Bloody hell!

Tina   Your eggs are in there.

She hands over the Lidl bag. **Tina** *kisses/hugs* **Rob**. **Florence** *locks the door and puts her key in her pocket.*

Florence   There's tea in the pot.

Tina   Smashing, Mum, thanks.

Florence *leaves.*

Rob   Is this enough wine?

Tina   Shut up you. Hi, Dad.

Jack   Aye.

Tina   How are you?

Florence (*serving hatch*)   He's coughing up rubbish.

Jack   She asked me, not you!

Tina   What colour do –

Florence (*serving hatch*)   – brown with red specks!

Rob   He won't go for an X-ray.

Tina   GP first.

Rob   That's pretty good going from Taunton.

Jack   She speeds!

Tina   Nought to sixty in two and a half seconds. Electric.

Rob   Jeez.

Jack   You wouldn't speed if you'd ever had to go to a crash.

Florence (*serving hatch*)   Why do you speed then? Fifty in a thirty limit!

Jack   I had a drop in blood pressure, that's why I went through that hedge.

Florence (*serving hatch*)   At fifty mile an hour.

Jack   Thirty!

Florence (*serving hatch*)   Fifty!

Tina   Still on that one, are we?

Rob   It's a mini series.

Tina   I'll get my things in.

She makes for the door. It's locked. She can't get out.

It's locked!

Florence *can't find the key. She starts looking for it.* **Rob** *looks in the kitchen.*

Tina   I'll sit and have me tea.

Florence (*serving hatch*)   The fish pie's in the oven.

Enter **Florence** *from kitchen.*

Jack   Oh no. Fish pie. Again.

Florence   We only have fish pie once a week.

Jack   That's fifty-two times a year! Do you think they have fish pie fifty-two times a year in heaven?

Tina   I love your fish pie, Mum.

Florence   You can have your dad's then.

Rob   So whose key is this?

Tina   Must be Mum's.

Jack   We gave you both a front door key three years ago.

Tina   We've both got keys, have we?

Jack   You won't remember, because you don't care.

Tina   I'm here, look at me, I care.

Jack   At the rate you visit, twice a year, you'll see your mother ten times before she dies.

Florence   How long's he giving me?

Rob   Five years.

Jack   You left us alone, went to Somerset. He went to America.

Rob   London.

Tina   We're here now.

Jack   Too late.

Florence   We're the first generation that never see their kids.

Rob   You gave us the opportunity of an education and –

Jack   – and that took you away forever.

Tina   Driffield is –

Jack   – not big enough for your business, I know.

Florence   Folks round here won't pay to see a doctor.

Rob   And there's no film industry in Wetwang.

Tina   Jesus, this is heavy talk. I've hardly sat down.

Rob (*to* **Tina**)   Do you have a key?

Tina   No.

Florence   You have to be able to get in if he's dead on the floor.

Jack   If I'm dead on the floor but you're still buzzing around like a blue-arsed fly, they don't need a key, do they.

Florence   If you're dead on the floor, I won't be here I'll be off on a cruise!

Jack   I give 'em both keys in case you're dead an' all.

Florence   If we're both dead?

Jack   Yes! If the house is locked and we're both inside, dead on the floor.

Florence   What are the chances of that?!

Jack   It's very common, in long lasting marriages, that when one half goes the other goes soon after.

Florence   Not ten minutes after.

Jack   Soon after!

Florence   That only happens with couples who like each other.

Rob   What if Mum dies first?

Tina   Good point.

Florence   If I go first, are you planning on dying ten minutes after?!

Jack   I will, yes, if only to prove you wrong!

Rob (*to* **Tina**)   So, if that's what happens, you've got a key.

Rob *gives* **Tina** *a key.*

Tina   I can get out now.

Inexplicably, she opens a window first and then lets herself out the front door.

Jack   What's she doing? Opening that window?

Florence   Do you want tea, Jack?

Jack   Tea, tea, tea bloody tea! No!

Tina *sticks her head through the window.*

Tina   Rob, could you give me a hand?

Jack   What is she doing?

Tina *hands to* **Rob** *a fat car charging cable/power pack. She feeds it through the window.*

Tina   There's a plug socket over there.

Rob (*smile on his face*)   Dad?

Rob *looks at his dad.*

Jack   What the hell is going on?!

Tina *sticks her head through the open window.*

Tina   I'm charging the Tesla.

End of scene.

Saturday

Scene Two

Front stage. **Tina** *and* **Rob** *are sitting on a garden bench, before them is an open bottle of St. Emilion Grand Cru.* **Rob***, pretentiously, swirls his wine and sniffs.*

Rob   Not bad.

Tina   Drink it first!

He drinks and then looks at the bottle.

Rob   St. Emilion. Grand Cru?!

Tina   Lidl. Twelve ninety-nine.

Rob   Grand Cru, for twelve ninety-nine? Bollocks.

Tina   Instead of milk, Lidl use Grand Cru as a loss leader.

Rob   In Waitrose that would be at least –

Tina   – stop! You're in Waitrose! By merely walking in there you've agreed to be taken up the arse!

Rob   Cheers.

They drink.

Mum's eyesight?

Tina   She feels for the hot plates on the hob.

Rob   She can see well enough to catch Dad watching porn.

Tina   Oh no! I don't want to know.

Rob   Through the hatch. On screen a naked woman, full frontal. Vagewelry; pierced nipples; tattoos.

Tina   What time of day?

Rob   Evening. They don't have a DVD player, I can't believe he's subscribed to a porn channel. I can't work it out.

Tina   What day of the week was it?

Rob   Yesterday. Friday. About nine.

Tina   Channel Four?

Rob   Who knows?

Tina   *Naked Attraction.*

Rob *puts his head in his hands and groans.*

Rob   Of course! The bastards! Do you know what fucks me off about Channel Four is that whoever came up with *Naked Attraction*, I guarantee you they went to Oxford and their preferred entertainment is outdoor opera in Tuscany. Ruining my parents' marriage. Thoughtless bastards!

Tina   I'll explain it to Mum, leave it to me, anything to do with vaginas.

They drink.

Rob   If they sell up and move in with you, you know what that means?

Tina   I'm living with my mum and dad again.

Rob   Could you?

Tina   Yes. I'm never there. I'm planning an invasion of Australia. I'm setting up a pilot practice in Melbourne, if that goes well I might stay forever.

Rob   They use sandpaper to cheat at cricket.

Tina   What's important to me is that Australians don't mind paying for private GP services, unlike the Brits.

Rob   So how's it work?

Tina   It's like a gym membership, a monthly payment, and the beauty is, a bit like gym membership, no one ever goes.

Rob   Money for nothing.

Tina   And your chicks for free.

Rob   What happens if one of your members falls ill?

Tina   Members falling ill is the only real threat to the success of the business. People thinking they've got athlete's foot is our Achilles heel. Is that the right way round?

Rob   Yup.

Rob   Are you happy?

Tina   No. It's all bloody achievement and I'm sick of it. I just want to stay in bed and grow strawberries.

Rob   In bed?

Tina   Yes.

Rob   The key to happiness is to love your obligations.

Tina   Which is why you're depressed.

Rob   Yup! Cheers!

They drink.

There's a word for people like you.

Tina   Beautiful sister?

Rob   Global villager. Someone who can live anywhere.

Tina   What are you?

Rob   I've been in Muswell Hill thirty-five years and I know two people, and they're both neighbours, and I don't like either of them. I want to live somewhere that cares about me, that would be lessened if I didn't live there.

Tina   Are you still online dating?

Rob   Yes. I'm sixty and getting 'favourited' by lots of seventy-year-old women.

Tina   Can't you say that you're looking for a fit, skinny, dark thirty-five-year-old?

Rob   No! You can't be honest about what you really want. It's Guardian Soulmates.

Tina   What happened to that fit, skinny, dark solicitor?

Rob   Gone.

Tina   The fit, skinny, dark earth scientist?

Rob   No.

Tina   The fit, skinny, dark philatelist?

Rob   Falangist.

Tina   What's a Falangist?

Rob   Kinda Spanish fascist.

Tina   I wondered why she didn't know anything about stamps.

Rob   I've got to learn to be more selfish.

Tina   If you make yourself happy that's one less person the state has to worry about.

Rob   Has rapacious capitalism made you happy?

Tina   Soft hearted rapacious capitalist global villager sister.

They drink.

Rob   You and Niall alright?

Tina   I need a hysterectomy.

Rob   Oh, OK, sorry to hear that.

Tina   Niall's anxious about it.

Rob   Has he never performed a hysterectomy?

Tina *knuckles him.*

Rob   Sorry! Just that Niall does all the plumbing in your house.

Tina   That's a yellow card.

They drink.

Rob   The granny flat will be great for Mum. But a man should die near his tools. And you can't play cricket for the Yorkshire Heaven eleven unless you die in Yorkshire.

Tina   Let's sell this house first.

Rob   Yup.

Tina   It's the bank I'm worried about. We've let them down there.

Rob   Badly. Can you hotspot with your phone and laptop?

Tina   Course.

Rob   If we break into the account, we're looking for ATM withdrawals –

Tina   – one after another.

Rob   A hundred followed by another hundred.

Tina   This could get ugly. Police.

Rob   Anyone stealing from my parents is going down.

Tina   Shit! Who'd have parents eh?

End of scene.

Saturday

Scene Three

After dinner, in the living room. **Jack** *in his chair,* **Florence** *on the sofa with* **Tina**, **Rob** *in the other chair.*

Jack   My will is under my bed.

Florence   No it isn't. It's in the safe under the stairs.

Jack   Since when?

Florence   Since I found it kicking around under the bed.

Jack   My will is in the safe under the stairs. It's one of them electric ones with a combination lock.

Tina   We'll need the combination.

Florence   The battery's flat so we leave the door open.

Jack   Whose speech is this?

Florence   I'm doing corrections.

Jack   It won't be long now before I buy the farm.

Florence   What's he buying?

Tina   It's a euphemism.

Florence   He's probably got one of them already.

Jack   Can I do my death bed speech without you interrupting!

Florence   You're not dying and you're not in bed.

Jack   I bloody am dying!

Florence   Hurry up then, no one's stopping you!

Tina   Mum! That's horrible.

Jack   I'm getting rid of the car.

Florence   Pam's looking for a car.

Jack   I'm not selling it to Pam!

Tina   What's it worth?

Jack   Nowt.

Tina   What are you worried about then?

Jack   I just spent two hundred quid on tyres.

Florence   He blamed the tyres when he drove through that hedge at fifty on the Scarborough Road.

Jack   Thirty!

Florence   I spent an hour in that ploughed field next to his dead body.

Jack   I was only unconscious and fifty wan't speeding.

Florence   In a thirty limit it is.

Jack   No one would ever get to bloody Scarborough if that road was a thirty limit.

Florence   It was like being tied to the front of a runaway train.

Jack   You've gorr an air bag!

Florence   Which you turned off! Like in the movies.

Jack   I wish you'd turn your airbag off! Them two hours I spent unconscious in that ploughed field is the only peace and quiet I've had in seventy years. Woke up to her working her way through a packet of classic Magnums.

Florence   They were melting.

Rob   It's a ten-year-old car.

Jack   It's a Lexus.

Rob   Toyota.

Jack   Luxury Toyota. With only eighteen thousand miles on the clock.

Florence   And it smells of pee.

Tina   Give it to Pam, Dad.

Jack   She's not getting one over me.

Florence   Have you finished?

Jack   I haven't started. I can't walk; we can't get to the shops; I can't even get to the gate; I can't get up the stairs; I can't get into the bath; I can't get out the bath; I can't open a jar; I can't get up if I fall over; I can't pick your mother up if she falls over. We can't look after ourselves no more. I've had a good life, but it's over now. I've lost all my work mates, all my friends, two brothers and a younger sister. There's only me left.

Florence   What am I then? The ship's cat?

Jack   I'm talking about the Kirks!

Florence   My name's Mrs Kirk.

Tina   Give him a chance.

Jack *reaches for some papers on top of the cabinet.*

Jack   These here forms, lasting power of attorney. You and Tina have a look, sign them, ready for when I'm not making sense any more.

Florence   That moment's been and gone.

Tina   Mother?!

Jack   All our savings are in premium bonds. I've got twenty thousand, and your mother's got twenty thousand. When I go –

Florence   – I get your twenty.

Jack   What?

Florence   I'm your wife, I get all your money.

Jack   That's not what I want!

Florence   You should've thought of that when you married me.

Rob   Mother!

Florence   What if I die first?

Jack   If you die first you get your own speech and I get all your money!

Florence   Speech?! I'd be dead.

Jack   We can't live here no more. We need to sell the house and move. I don't want to live in London or LA.

Florence   I'd quite like the swimming pool.

Jack   I'm a Yorkshireman, I don't want to live in Somerset, but given that neither of you live round here, I'm gonna have to bite the bullet. So this is why I asked you both home, to talk to your mother, see what she wants.

Tina   There are two rooms, private rooms for you in Somerset. The bedroom has an en-suite bathroom and toilet.

Florence   It's not a proper toilet.

Tina   How do you mean?

Florence   It's a whoosh one!

(*She does an impression.*) DRRRRRRRR! Whooooosh!

Jack   What the hell's she doing?

Rob   Quite an accurate impression of a food mixer toilet.

Florence   DRRRRRRR! Whoosh!

Tina   Macerating.

Jack   Fancy word. Education, education, education! That's what's destroyed this family.

Tina   This family is not destroyed, it's become an extended family, with a diaspora in Somerset and one in London via LA.

Jack   We're just two old people waiting to die. We never see you.

Rob (*quoting himself*)   There's no film industry in Wetwang.

Florence   That's why we like it.

Rob   If I was in the oil business I'd be in Aberdeen. I write, so I've ended up in London.

Jack   I'm not asking you to be a plumber and live round here.

Florence   But you'd do well, as a plumber, if you were any good. Round here.

Jack   What are you talking about now?!

Florence   You can't get a plumber round here for love for money.

Jack   For love, *nor* money.

Florence   What?

Rob   You can't get a plumber for love, nor money.

Florence   I don't even know what that means.

Rob   It means the plumber won't come out and fix your taps even if you offer to sleep with him!

Florence   I'm never saying that again then.

Rob *stands. The smoke alarm goes off.* **Rob** *rushes into the kitchen.*

Florence   Oh heck!

Jack   She's done it again!

Rob *rushes out to the kitchen.* **Florence** *follows.*

Jack   Three or four times a week this.

Tina   How's her eyesight?

Jack   Poor. When you get this old, everything's a test. I can't open a packet of peanuts.

Tina   Come and live with us. It'll be fun. Rob wants to record your police stories. That's a brilliant idea.

Jack   His idea. Not mine.

Rob *comes back in.* **Florence** *follows.*

Jack   Where were we before we nearly got burned out?

Tina   Selling the house.

Rob   Are you happy to sell up, Mum?

Florence   Yes. But I'm not moving.

Tina   When you sell a house you have to move out.

Florence   I'm talking about packing boxes.

Rob   We'll do that. And you'll go and live with Tina?

Florence   Will Niall be there?

Tina   My husband?

Florence   Yes, him.

Tina   He's my husband.

Florence   I'm only asking.

Jack   In other parts of the world the old are revered.

Florence   Go and live there then!

Tina   I'll find an estate agent, Tuesday, get the house valued.

Jack   Why not Monday?

Tina   I'm taking you to see a doctor.

Rob   I can find an estate agent.

Tina   No. Selling a house is a job for a rapacious capitalist.

Rob   Can we talk about money?

Jack   You've been treated equal. Tina's had an extra year for her wotsit –

Tina   – MBA.

Rob   Fire up the lappie.

Tina *starts to hotspot her laptop with her phone.*

Tina   We're going to try and look at your bank account.

Rob   We think Eddie might be stealing from you.

Florence   Eddie?! Na!

Jack   What makes you think that?

Rob   Let's try and get in the account first.

Rob *stands and looks over* **Tina**'*s shoulder.* **Tina** *types and clicks when necessary.*

Tina   Customer number.

Rob   Ten digits, made up of date of birth and a four-digit PIN –

Tina   – one-five-zero-four-two-eight.

Jack   Eh?

Rob   Your date of birth, Dad.

Florence   'Cept it isn't.

Jack   It's the only one on any clever paperwork.

Florence   I know things.

Tina   Mother, please!

Rob   Four-digit pin.

Jack   What's that?

Rob   A four-digit number that is your secret number, known only to you.

Florence   Six-eight-three-nine.

Jack   You're not supposed to know that!

Florence   That's his police number. He uses it for everything.

During the next sequence **Tina** *types in the letters and digits required.*

Tina   OK. Next.

Rob   Memorable word?

Tina   A word you wouldn't forget.

Jack   Elephant, banana, parsnip, bungalow, two pints of mild and a packet of crisps, please. I don't forget words!

Tina   A word you told the bank.

Jack   I didn't tell the bank anything.

Tina   With Pammy, did you write your memorable word down so you wouldn't forget it?

Jack   I can't remember.

Rob   Mum. Do you know his memorable word?

Florence   He knows his memorable word, he doesn't want to admit to it.

Jack   Robin Hoods Bay seven.

Tina   Oh.

Florence   Where we had our honeymoon.

Jack   Where I lost mi life.

Florence   Room seven. Sea view.

Jack   Only if you stood on the blanket box.

Tina   They want the fourth letter of that.

Rob   Lower case i.

Tina   Sixth letter.

Rob   Upper case aitch.

Tina   Seventh letter.

Rob   Lower case o.

Tina   Fourteenth.

Rob (*mental calculation, counting fingers*)   Er . . . seven, the number seven.

Tina   Ha! We're in.

Rob   Yes! OK. Do you want to know what your balance is?

Jack   We've got enough.

Florence   Should be about five thousand.

Tina   Two thousand seven hundred and eighty-four pounds, sixteen pence.

Jack   We've gorr enough!

Rob   Transactions.

Tina   Police pension.

Rob   Nice.

Florence   Do I get that when you're gone?

Jack   Yis! I don't know why. You didn't risk your life on the streets of Hull for twenty-five years.

Tina   State pension. Random debits. TV licence. Gas. Water. Council. Electric. DP ins. What's that? DP ins. Fifteen pounds a month.

Jack   Insurance against the washing machine.

Rob   Fifteen pounds a month?

Florence   It's working, it hasn't broken down yet.

Rob   Cash withdrawal, there.

Tina   One hundred.

Rob   Does Eddie always get out a hundred?

Jack   Aye. We know where we are with a hundred.

Florence   Every week.

Tina   Another one there, a hundred. No second withdrawal.

Rob   What's that direct debit?

Tina   GoCardless. Two hundred pounds. On the twenty-third of May.

Florence   Go-carts?

Rob   GoCardless. It's a direct debit service. Suki has drumming lessons every month and it's paid through GoCardless.

Florence (*to* **Jack**)   Are you having drumming lessons?

Jack   I thought you knew all my secrets.

Rob   Look at April.

Tina   Yes. Every month. GoCardless. Two hundred pounds.

Rob   No?

Jack   Never heard of it.

Rob   Go to the GoCardless website.

Florence   What are you buying on my joint account that costs two hundred every month?

Jack   There's no such thing as 'my joint account'. Anyone who says the sentence 'my joint account' doesn't understand banking.

Rob   Now click on their payment look up tool. I did this for Suki's drumming. I'd forgotten about it. And I just saw GoCardless every month, didn't know what it was.

Florence   Have you got a fancy woman?

Jack   I don't even have the energy for an allotment, never mind a fancy woman!

Florence   Maybe warfarin has side effects.

Rob   That means the joint account account number.

Tina *refers to a cheque book and taps in the account number.*

Rob   Then the amount, two hundred.

Tina *does that.*

Rob   That's it, there.

Tina   Oh no.

Jack   What have you got?

Tina   The direct debit every month for two hundred pounds.

Rob   Rhubarb Fool Ltd.

Interval.

Sunday

Sunday morning, before midday. **Jack** *is in his chair, in pyjamas and dressing gown. By his chair, on an occasional table, is a plate of Jacobs Cream Crackers and thin slices of Cheddar cheese. On his knee is a small cassette tape recorder. He presses Play, watches for the leader to run out, presses Stop. He presses Record and Play.*

Jack The Wedding Dress. I was on nights, 'bout 1958, me and Hopalong, Inspector Arnold . . . he's dead. We'd been called out to a body in Foredyke Stream. It was a woman, 'bout forty, floating face up like lasses do. Dyed yellow hair, look of terror on her face, wearing a wedding dress. Always upsets me this one. Bugger! We pulled the body into the bank. Lifting her out one of her bosoms fell out. It had 'Mild' tattooed on it. So, because I had a good excuse, I had a look at the other one, and it had 'Bitter' tattooed on it, so I knew we was dealing with maybe not the highest class of person in East Hull. The post mortem said she'd been murdered. Choked and then chucked in the dyke. But who was she? Everyone, no matter how desperate their lifestyle, has someone who needs them. I put a missing person's report out to all stations. Ten minutes later, aye, ten minutes later, the Clough Road desk sergeant said he had two girls in, a six-year-old and a seven-year-old, saying their mum hadn't come home. I went down Clough Road nick and got the kids to describe their mum, and, unfortunately, we had a match. Alice Cookham, street prostitute. But she'd never married, so it weren't her wedding dress. Wedding dresses are usually bespoke, methinks. I hawk it around all the dress shops but no one claimed to have made it. Someone said the lobster clasp on the back was unusual. They helped me go through the trade catalogues and we found the the supplier, Samuel Bees, Todmorden. Rang up and they told us they supplied hundreds of dress makers but the nearest to Hull was Bridlington . . . argh bugger . . . what's her name?

He presses Pause. Thinks. Presses Pause again.

Kate Bambridge Bespoke. I drove out with the dress. Yeah,
Kate had designed it, a beautiful bride, about twenty-eight,
slim, well spoken. She found the carbon copy of the invoice.
Sarah Becks was the bride, from Carnaby Village. I went
straight there, and it's her parents', innit. They tell me she
married a lad called Alan Miles, an accountant with Plaxton's
the coach makers in Scarborough. Her mother looked at the
floor as she told me that after six months' marriage she ran
off with a Norwegian ship's captain. I'm thinking if I were to
run off with a Norwegian sailor I might just leave mi
wedding dress with mi husband. Scarborough's only up the
road, so even though I'm on my own, go to their nick, tell
them I need to make an arrest and I don't want to be on mi
tod. They give me three woodentops and a van, and we go
to Plaxton's. I ask for Alan Miles at reception and the girl
walks me to his office, with the three uniforms behind.
Everyone stops work and watches. The four of us go into his
office. He was a big, powerful, rugby type. His left ear was
bandaged. He says 'Do you mind if we go out down the fire
escape. I don't want to walk through the office.' He had tears
in his eyes. We cuffed him and that was that. Pleaded guilty.
He still loved his wife and he'd got into habit of making
working girls wear the wedding dress, but Alice's tattoos had
disgusted him and he hit her. She bit his ear off and in the
heat of it all, he broke her neck. I know what you're
thinking, it's a schoolboy error to dispose of a body in a
bespoke wedding dress. But most people, unless they're
born evil, actually want to get caught.

There is the noise of a car.

. . . bugger! Thank you.

*He stops the tape, ejects it, puts it in a case, and into the cabinet, the
door of which he locks. He puts another cassette into the player and
presses play. It's Jim Reeves singing 'Goodnight Irene'. He turns the
television on but with the sound off. The programme is* Bargain

Hunt. *A key in the lock. The lock turns. Enter* **Rob**, *carrying two Lidl carrier bags.*

Rob   Alright, Dad?

Jack   Aye.

Rob *goes through to the kitchen with the shopping. Enter* **Tina** *helping* **Florence** *over the step.* **Tina** *closes the door.* **Florence** *locks it, putting her key in her coat pocket.* **Tina** *kicks her shoes off and sits in the armchair downstage right.*

Florence   What's he watching?

Jack *turns Jim Reeves and 'Goodnight Irene' off.*

Jack   *Bargain Hunt.*

Florence   You don't like *Bargain Hunt.* You think they're all prats.

Jack   They are all prats, that's what's entertaining.

Tina   You've got the sound off, Dad.

Jack   I was playing Jim Reeves.

Florence   I thought the singing was on the telly.

Jack   Jim Reeves in't gonna be on *Bargain Hunt,* he's dead.

Florence   He couldn't have kids, Jim Reeves. Mumps.

Tina   He had what?

Florence   Mumps!

Jack   That's all she knows about Jim Reeves. His bloody mumps.

Tina   Jim Reeves was sterile was he?

Florence   Yes. Mumps.

Jack   What was it?

Florence   Mumps! You know it was mumps!

Rob   How do mumps make you sterile?

Florence   Inflammation of his . . . whatsits.

Jack   Testicles!

Florence   No need to swear.

Tina   I thought he died in a plane crash.

Jack   He was the pilot!

Florence   It didn't kill him.

Jack   You don't walk away from a plane crash.

Florence   It weren't the mumps that killed him!

Jack   Will you stop saying 'the mumps', 'the mumps'. It's like a madhouse!

Tina   So Jim Reeves died in a plane crash –

Jack   – with inflamed testicles, from the mumps, which were uncomfortable, so he was adjusting his tackle when he crashed.

Rob   So the mumps did kill him.

Florence   The mumps didn't kill him! Mumps can't –

Tina   – can we all stop saying mumps! Please! Maybe a cup of tea?

Florence   Do you want a cup of tea?

Jack   Do I look like I want a cup of tea?!

Florence   Is that a 'no' then?

Jack   Yes!

Florence   'Yes' or 'No'?

Jack   No?!

Florence   Why do you keep changing your mind?!

Jack   I haven't changed my mind!

Florence   I'll make you one then.

Jack   I don't want tea ever again!

Florence   What about you Rob, Tina? Tea?

Rob   Yes please, Mum.

Florence   Are you going to get dressed today?

Jack   Sunday is wear what you like day in Wetwang!

Florence   You make the house look like an Old People's Home.

Jack   It is an old people's home!

Tina   I was expecting a smell of brisket.

Florence   I knew I'd forgotten something!

Tina   You said you were going to slow cook it.

Florence   I was but that Crock-Pot's too slow.

Jack   It's a slow cooker.

Florence   What I need is a fast slow cooker.

Enter **Rob**. **Florence** *exits to the kitchen.*

Jack   I've had nearly seventy years of this. You can't have a fast slow cooker!

Rob   If you have a race between ten snails, it's the fast one that wins.

Jack   Education, education, education! I stayed in Yorkshire. Look at me. Stupid.

Jack *starts coughing.* **Florence** *opens the hatch.*

Florence (*through the hatch*)   Is he coughing again? Robert, Tina, can you have a listen to his lungs?

Tina   I'm not a doctor!

Florence (*through the hatch*)   I thought you ran a doctor's surgery.

Tina   I run fifteen doctors' surgeries but I'm the business manager. He's seeing a GP tomorrow.

Jack   Who am I seeing?

Tina   A doctor. We have a partner franchise in Scarborough.

Florence (*through the hatch*)   He won't go if it's private.

Tina   He's no choice. I'm having someone listen to those lungs.

Jack   Who are we all talking about?

Florence (*through the hatch*)   You. You're going to Scarborough tomorrow.

Jack   Are you going?

Florence (*through the hatch*)   There's nowt wrong with me.

Jack   Do you want a second opinion? I'll get three hours off then.

Florence (*through the hatch*)   Off what?

Jack   Off you!

Florence *closes the hatch.*

Jack   Where's my cup of tea?

Florence (*through the hatch*)   Oh, you want one now, do you?

Jack   I didn't want one half an hour ago when you fost asked.

Florence *closes the hatch. The phone rings. She opens the hatch.*
Jack *picks the phone up.*

Jack   Hello!

There is kicking on the bottom of the door between the living room and the kitchen.

Florence (*off*)   Can you open this door someone? I've got a tray in my hand.

Jack   Hang on, luv, I can't hear a thing.

Tina *opens the door for* **Florence** *and takes the tray off of her.* **Florence** *picks the other phone up.* **Jack** *having seen her pick the phone up, puts his end down.* **Rob** *leaps in and stops* **Florence** *putting her phone down.*

Florence (*posh voice*)   Wetwang double-two three-five . . . oh it's you, Pammy . . . yes . . . yes . . . yes . . . yes.

Jack   Yes . . . yes . . . yes . . . yes.

Florence   Shut up! (*On phone.*) Not you, Pammy. Him.

(*To* **Jack**.) She wants to test drive the car tomorrow.

Jack   No. I'm going to Scarborough.

Tina   We're going in my car.

Jack   Yes. She can. Take no notice of me. I'm old and stupid, and I didn't know there were fast snails.

Rob   I'll be here.

Florence (*on phone*)   Rob will be here . . . the car has got some bits of hedge sticking out of the radiator and it smells of pee.

Jack   Basically it's a crime scene!

Florence (*on phone*)   He won't want much for it . . .

Jack   I bloody do!

Doorbell.

Florence   That's the door now!

Rob *stands and tries the door which is locked.*

Rob   It's locked.

Florence (*on the phone*)   Hang on, Pammy.

She puts the phone down, cutting **Pamela** *off.* **Florence** *looks for her key.*

Jack   In your pinny!

Florence *with* **Rob**'s *help opens the door.*

Jack   Who is it?

Eddie (*off*)   It's me!

Florence   Oh. It's Eddie.

Florence *picks the phone up.*

(*On the phone.*) Sorry, Pam, they're going to the hospital for ten –

Jack   – she's gone.

Florence   Did you put your end down?

Jack   You put your end down. I didn't have my end up!

Eddie, *in socks, comes in. He is carrying a plastic shopping bag.* **Tina** *and* **Rob** *swap looks.*

Eddie   How do?

Jack   Come in, Eddie. You're very welcome.

Tina *stands, vacating the down stage right chair.*

Tina   I'm Tina.

Eddie   Eddie.

Florence   We call him Rhubarb Eddie.

Tina   To differentiate from some other Eddie?

Florence   No. That's just his name.

Eddie *sits in the chair and flicks the footrest controls. He flies up.*

Eddie   Wahey!

Florence   He loves that!

Jack   What are you hiding in that bag?

Eddie   Mi latest invention.

Florence   He's invented some stuff has Eddie.

Jack   Bigger hands.

Tina   Bigger hands?

Eddie   Have you never wished you had bigger hands?

Tina   Er . . .

Rob   Picking up leaves hands?

Eddie   Aye. On'y mine weren't plastic.

Tina   They sell them in garden centres.

Rob   That was you was it, Eddie?

Eddie   Mine was marine ply. And a leather belt on each one, for your hands.

Jack   Weighed a ton.

Tina   Did you protect it with a patent?

Eddie   No, linseed oil.

Florence   Linseed oil! Ha, ha. He's ever so funny.

Jack   What's today's invention then?

Eddie   'Doom fly!'

Jack   Bloody flies everywhere.

Eddie *dives into his bag and brings out a rat glue strip. He peels off the backing paper.*

Eddie   Rat glue sticky strip.

Florence   We 'an't got rats!

Eddie   The rat stands on that and he's stuck, can't get off.

Jack   I know how he feels.

Eddie   Component number two, is the gun.

Florence   A gun?!

Eddie *dives into his bag and comes up with a plumber's compressed air gun.*

Eddie   Plumber's compressed air gun. Ten ninety-nine.

He starts pumping it.

You pump it up. Now all we need is a fly.

Rob   There's one on Dad's crackers.

Jack *picks up his fly swatter.*

Eddie   No, Jack! We need the fly.

Eddie *creeps up on the fly with the gun in his right hand and the glue strip in his left.*

Eddie   So you get the glue strip behind the fly, slowly, gently. Then the compressed air gun –

Rob   – you're trying to blow the fly on to the glue strip.

Eddie   Aye. Very quiet.

Eddie *creeps up on the fly. He fires the gun and the cheese and crackers go everywhere.*

Jack   Mi crackers! Mi cheese!

Florence   They're all over the floor!

Eddie   Got it!

Jack   I 'an't had any of them yit!

Eddie   See?!

Eddie *holds up the rat strip which shows the fly on it and maybe some crackers too.*

Florence   The little bugger's still alive! Kill it!

Eddie   I never bother.

Florence   Kill it!

Eddie *stands on the glue strip which sticks to his sock.*

Eddie   Agh! Bloody hell.

He stomps around trying to kick off the rat strip but the sock is fast. He tears his sock off his foot but the sock is still stuck the rat trap.

Florence (*laughing*)   He's so funny!

Jack   One glue strip, one gun and one pair of socks for every fly.

Eddie   D'yer see the principle?

Jack   Principle? The word I'd use is 'chaos'.

Eddie   D'yer think I could patent it?

Rob   Comedy is copyright.

Florence   I'll get you some socks.

Florence *gets up and heads for the kitchen.*

Eddie   I've got mi wellies outside.

Florence   You can't wear wellies with no socks, you'll get wellie foot.

Florence *exits to the kitchen.*

Jack   Have you got mi money?

Eddie   Aye.

He takes out a hundred in twenties and tens.

A hundred, cash.

*He gives the money to **Jack**, who counts it himself.*

Jack   Receipt.

Eddie *starts looking for the receipt.*

Eddie   Curry, curry –

Jack   – you do that gag every time, I'm sick of it! I don't need a receipt.

Tina   I'd like the receipt please.

Eddie *looks at* **Tina**, *unsettled. He gives her the receipt.* **Florence** *returns from the kitchen with a pair of socks.*

Eddie   Who's having the card?

Jack   Me!

Florence   Me. Tina's got yours. And you don't know the PIN.

Jack   I've got it written down.

Florence   You're not supposed to write it down. You don't write the PIN down do you, Eddie?

Eddie   No.

Florence   He might look stupid but he's not.

Jack   He's got three allotments, he has to be a bloody genius.

Florence   Did you ever go to school, Eddie?

Eddie   Aye, I did. Twice. The educational psychologist said I was . . . what is it –

Jack   – dyslexic?!

Eddie   No.

Jack   Autistic?

Eddie   No.

Jack   What did she say you was?

Eddie   Really thick.

Florence   Ha, ha! And her a scientist.

Jack   These are old jokes of his.

Tina   I'd like to talk to you about money, Eddie.

Eddie   Aye?

Jack   Rob, there's your fifty, for petrol. Tina, your fifty.

Both of them get up and collect their money.

Eddie   He gives you petrol money? For coming home?

Rob   We don't ask for it.

Eddie   Queer.

Rob   In what sense queer, Eddie?

Eddie   They're your mum and dad.

Tina   We are given it.

Eddie   Rum business.

Tina   Rhubarb Fool Ltd.

Florence   Oh no.

Eddie   What?

Rob   Rhubarb Fool Ltd.

Eddie   Who are they then? Forcing sheds are they?

Tina   You're denying it?

Eddie   What is this, Jack?

Jack   Nowt to do wi me.

Rob   Do you have any involvement with Rhubarb Fool Ltd?

Eddie   Where are they based?

Tina   Pocklington.

Florence   I put some socks there for you, Eddie luv.

Eddie   Thanks, Flo.

Eddie *takes the socks.*

Jack   Let me see them.

Eddie *shows the socks.*

Jack   You can't give him them.

Florence   Why not?

Jack   They're not mine. They're Bobby Bennet's.

Florence   He's dead.

Jack   Yes, he is dead but they're still his socks!

Florence   What are we doing with a dead man's socks?

Jack   He loaned them to us when mine got wet. I said I'd post them back to him.

Florence   What's he gonna do with them now that he's dead?

Jack   It's the principle, I'm a man of mi word!

Florence   Tek 'em, Eddie.

Jack   Yeah, yeah, ignore me, they're yours now.

Eddie   I don't want –

Jack   – tek 'em, Bobby's dead, and when you're dead you're nothing, people can nick your stuff, give your socks away, rip out yer kidneys for science, grind your bones down into fertiliser, tek 'em, Eddie, they're yours.

Eddie   I'll manage. I've got mi wellies.

Tina   Can we get back to money, please?

Eddie   What is it?

Tina   My parents are paying two hundred pounds a month to a company in Pocklington called Rhubarb Fool Ltd.

Eddie   That meks no sense, 'cause I give 'em free rhubarb. Don't I, Flo?

Florence   Yes you do, luv.

Eddie   Because your dad give us his allotment.

Florence   We get lots of beautiful free rhubarb, Tina.

Jack   Too much. I'm sick of it.

Eddie   Why would they pay for rhubarb?

Tina   They're not knowingly paying for rhubarb.

Eddie   That's a lot of rhubarb, two hundred a month.

Rob   You're denying it?

Eddie   Denying what?

Rob   Did you set up a direct debit from their bank account to Rhubarb Fool Ltd?

Eddie   Do I look like a limited company? I do deny it. And, I don't live in Pocklington, I live in Wetwang. Jack?

Jack   I'm not accusing you, Eddie. It's the internet. It's their world.

Eddie *stands, as if to leave.*

Eddie   D'yer see that? I've stood up.

Florence   Take the socks, luv.

Eddie   No ta. Are you . . . you are, aren't you. Me, steal money from your mum and dad? Bloody hell. You know, I call in here three maybe four times a week. Bring 'em cash. Bit of shopping.

Jack   Cod liver oil.

Eddie   Allsorts.

Jack   Epoxy resin.

Florence   Rubber gloves.

Jack   Sunglasses.

Eddie   Owt they need from Driffield.

Jack   Liquorice Allsorts.

Eddie   Wetwang post office don't have much.

Florence   Stamps.

Eddie   And I keep 'em company. I come here for his stories. I'm gonna go before I get upset. I know when I'm not wanted.

Eddie *glares at them, accusingly and makes to leave.*

Florence   Bye, luv.

Eddie *leaves.*

Jack   Well done, everybody. You've just hanged the wrong man.

End of scene.

Monday

The next day, a Monday. Mid morning. **Jack** *in his chair and* **Rob** *on the sofa.* **Rob** *is looking at his phone.*

Jack   That's what human beings look like now, in't it. Head down, spine bent, like a cripple, staring at a little telly. Robots.

Rob   Harsh.

Jack   Tina was here last summer and lost her phone. You'd think a child had died.

Rob   Yup.

Jack   She took us to Bridlington. Next to us, on the beach, there's mum, dad and two teenagers, all four of them was staring at a phone. The ocean, before them, ignored. What's his name?

Rob   Who?

Jack   The fellah who owns all the internet.

Rob   Jeff Bezos, Bill Gates, Steve Jobs, Mark Zuckerberg.

Jack   Zuckerberg. There's kids out there with criminal records for nicking a Mars bar; Zuckerberg's ruined the world and he's walking around scot-free.

Rob   No one ever died in a train crash before the invention of trains.

Jack   Progress, aye.

Rob   But I'm with you, Dad. I bought a new toilet brush, off Amazon, about a month ago, since then I'm inundated with pop up ads for toilet brushes. I'm going to write to their algorithm and tell them I'm not a toilet brush collector.

Jack   What are you writing at the moment? Film?

Rob   No. Another Inspector Jenus. An arson murder.

Jack   We had one of them once. Coltman Street.

Rob   Rough area.

Jack   The fire was out by time I got there. Found this Dutchman, dead in bed.

Rob   How did you know he was Dutch?

Jack   Neighbours. He worked nights at Jackson's and slept until three in the afternoon. The living room was untouched by the fire and I found a candle set on a copy of the *Grimsby Evening Telegraph*.

Rob   Ah! Delayed incendiary?

Jack   Hardly ever works and this one didn't. But he'd set two others, one of which had worked, candle on a newspaper. So I thought who the hell, in Hull, reads the *Grimsby Evening Telegraph*?

Rob   Someone from Grimsby.

Jack   Turns out the Dutch lad had given this sixteen-year-old Grimsby lass a bun in the oven and done a runner.

Rob   Sex or money.

Jack   There's nowt else. Her father –

Rob   – the arsonist, murderer.

Jack   Killed him by burning the house down knowing he'd be sleeping.

Rob   Stupid. Using a Grimsby newspaper.

Jack   People are stupid. If you want to kill the lad, kill him, don't leave your name and address at the crime scene.

Rob   Seriously, Dad, we have to get these stories down.

Jack   I'm not dead yet.

Enter **Florence**.

Florence   What's he on about now?

Rob   Coltman Street.

Florence   The fire? The one who had it off with that lass in Lincoln.

Jack   Grimsby!

Florence   Lincoln, Grimsby, what's the difference?

Jack   One's gorra cathedral, t'other's gorra fish dock!

Rob   Trying to get Dad to let me record his stories.

Florence   Ask me, I've heard 'em all fifty times.

Jack   Sammy Eccles, traffic officer –

Florence (*to* **Rob**)   Do you remember Sammy Eccles?

Rob   I do. You're going to tell me he's dead.

Florence   He's not dead.

Rob   Thank God for that.

Florence   He's in a coma.

Jack   Who's telling this story?!

Florence   You are. You missed out he's in a coma.

Jack   Afore he was in a coma, he put all his memoirs down in a book. Six pound ninety-nine.

Rob   Vanity publishing?

Jack   No, he had to pay all the printing costs hissen. Dunno how many copies he shifted. Don't matter now.

Rob   Why?

Florence   'Cause he's in a coma.

Jack   You already told us he's in a coma!

Rob   But his book lives on!

Jack   He made it all up!

Florence   Do you want a –

Jack   – no! And neither does he!

Florence   I'm only asking.

Florence *sits.*

Florence   His head's full of nutters, murders, rapes. It's like living with wotshisname.

Jack   Who?!

Florence   The films fellah. Director.

Jack   Steven Spielberg! Martin Scorsese. Quentin Tarantino –

Florence   – the one I'm thinking of did that one where a lass gets killed.

Rob   Who was the actress?

Jack   Meryl Streep. Brigitte Bardot. Grace Kelly. Hayley Mills. Bo Derrick. Hilda Baker.

Florence   Always had a fur coat.

Jack   Lassie!

Florence   She was married to that fella who was in that film with his friend who had a sailor's hat on –

Jack   – Popeye!

Florence   The fella with the hat falls in love with that actress who married the fella with the glasses.

Jack   Alf Garnett! John Lennon!

Florence   He wrote plays! She had a dress that went up and down and showed her knickers.

Rob   Marilyn Monroe! Arthur Miller!

Florence   Yes!

Rob   Living with Dad is like living with Arthur Miller?

Florence   No! The actor what was in love with Marilyn Monroe was in the film where he had to dress up like a woman.

Jack   Danny La Rue! Lily Savage!

Florence   His friend –

Rob   – in the film?

Florence   – yes, oh what's his name, like a fruit.

Rob   Jack Lemmon! *Some Like it Hot*! Tony Curtis!

Florence   That's him!

Rob   So living with Dad is like living with Tony Curtis?

Florence   No, Tony Curtis married the girl who's killed in the film what's directed by the fella who, if I lived with him, would be like living with your dad.

Jack   That doesn't help!

Florence   Why not?!

Jack   Tony Curtis was married six times!

Rob   I'll Google it.

Jack (*fiercely*)   No! No. No. I'm not having it. We can do this. This is our problem.

Silence. They think.

(*Quietly.*) Janet Leigh.

Florence   Yes! She was stabbed in the shower.

Jack   Psycho.

Rob   Alfred Hitchcock!

Florence   Yes! Living with him is like what living with Alfred Hitchcock would be like.

Florence *exits to the kitchen and closes the door with a bang. The stair lift beeps into action.*

Jack   I need a cup of tea now, I'm exhausted.

Enter **Tina** *down the stair lift wearing a coat and carrying a laptop case.*

Tina (*from the stair lift*)   Keep the noise down, please!

Rob   Bit of a lexical Easter egg hunt.

Jack   Searching for Alfred Hitchcock.

Rob   Mum's clue was Some Like it Hot.

Tina   Hitchcock didn't direct that.

Jack   When your mother's looking for summat she starts in outer space.

Doorbell. **Tina** *goes to the door. She tries it, it's locked.*

Tina   Locked!

Enter **Florence**.

Florence   Who is it?

Jack   It's locked!

Florence   Where's mi key?

Jack   In your pocket!

Rob *stands.*

Rob   I have a key.

He opens the door.

It's Pammy.

Enter **Pamela***, in her usual work uniform, she is carrying several pages of A4 print outs containing PDFs of the bank account.*

Pamela   Hello, Tina. Been ages.

Tina   Yes. Couple of years.

Florence   You should be at work shouldn't you, Pammy?

Pamela   I'm on at two. And then the evening shift.

Rob   You'd like to test drive the car?

Pamela   Is that alright, Jack?

Jack   I'm gonna the doctor's, against my will. Rob's in charge. Cost me eight and a half thousand.

Pamela   Ten years ago. Second hand.

Jack   I told you she'd haggle.

Tina *picks* **Jack***'s coat off the rack.*

Tina   We need to go.

Jack *laboriously hoists himself up.* **Rob** *stands and offers his arm.*

Florence   Give him his stick.

Jack   I've got three hours ahead of me with no stick from you.

Florence   Make the most of it.

Jack *puts his coat on, helped by* **Tina**. **Florence** *puts the bank statements on the cabinet.*

Pamela   Tina. I printed out the bank statements, like you asked.

Tina   Good. Thanks.

Pamela   I've always shown them on the iPad.

Tina   Mum can't see.

Pamela   I know. And Jack's not interested. Which is why I stopped.

Tina   They should've had printed statements.

Pamela   I set it up for them.

Tina   Sorry, what I meant was –

Pamela   – you should've set it up for them but you weren't here.

Tina   I'm not criticising you.

Rob   We should've known the bank had closed down.

Pamela   I wrote down all the passwords and PINs for them. I thought you could post print outs to them from Somerset.

Rob   The bank have to provide printed statements by post, if you ask.

Pamela   Yes, but I can't request statements because I'm not them. He has to do it for himself, and he can never get past security. Isn't that right, Uncle Jack?

Jack *heads for the door.*

Jack   I'm going!

Tina   Thank you, Pammy, for everything. If we owe you for –

Pamela   – the paper?

Tina   Milk, petrol, paper.

Rob   We don't want you to be out of pocket.

Pamela   I'm not interested in money. It's family.

Tina   But you're not our family, your my mother's sister's family.

Pamela   Nanna wouldn't think like that.

Tina   Nanna died thirty years ago. See you later. Wish us luck.

Florence   Bye!

Jack *and* **Tina** *exit.* **Florence** *closes the door intent on locking it.*

Rob   Please, Mum! Don't lock the door.

Pamela   Is there a problem with the bank?

Rob   Yes. There is.

Pamela   What is it?

Rob   I'd rather not talk about it.

Florence   Eddie's been stealing from us.

Pamela   I didn't like him having the card. I said.

Florence   I'll miss him.

Pamela   They sit here and chat. Jack's probably told him all his PINs.

Rob   Yup! Test drive. That's you driving then?

Pamela   Be stupid any other way.

Rob   It would be stupid if I drove yes, stupid but legal. I'm a policeman's son. Let's break the law, eh. Let's have you driving which would be sensible but illegal.

Pamela *heads for the door.*

Rob   Won't be long, Mum. I'll put the telly on. What do you want to watch?

Florence *sits.*

Florence   *Police Interceptors*.

Rob *presses the remote until* Motorway Cops *comes on.*

Rob   This is *Motorway Cops*. It's much the same.

Florence   They'll do.

The telly blares out Cops *soundtrack.*

Pamela   See you in a bit, Flo.

Florence   Turn the air bag on.

Pamela   I'm driving!

Door closes. **Florence** *uses the remote to turn the* Motorway Cops *noises up.* **Florence***'s eyes turn to the cabinet. She tries the door. It's locked. She sits down again. Watches TV.*

End of scene.

Tuesday

It's late afternoon. **Jack** *is on his own. He has his tape recorder on his lap. He puts the tape into the cassette. He presses Play to move the tape along. He ejects the tape, looks at it, to see that he's on the brown and not the leader, then presses Play and Record simultaneously.*

Jack   The Genius. I left school at fourteen and was apprenticed to Calvert's, as a farrier, blacksmith. Early on he loaned me out to an agricultural engineer called Dan North. Dan was a genius, no training, self-taught, owt to do with metal. He had three men working for him fixing agricultural equipment. One day, he took me out to a farm near Sproatley. They had a standing engine for driving conveyor belts and the aluminium casing had cracked open. It was shot. Dan drilled three holes either side of the crack and tapped a thread into each and with bolts he run metal straps across the crack. He was stitching metal. The farmer fired up the engine and, I were gobsmacked, it worked. I did a year with him and when I left he was employing eight men and the business was flying. Jump to twenty years later. I get a call in the nick. It's Dan. He says 'Hello Jack, have you got a moment?' I said 'No, I'm in court in ten minutes, I'll drive out, see you Saturday.' Saturday, I drove into his yard, and I knew summat was wrong 'cause it was quiet, the opposite of how I remembered it. Dan said one of his workers fell off a lorry, cracked a vertebrae and sued him for negligence. He was bankrupt. 'I'm in a bad place Jack, mentally.' We had a walk round his plot, talked about the old days. When I got home I rang his house, knowing that his wife would answer. I told her to get rid of his guns. She promised me she'd take his two shotguns to her brother's. A week later, the phone rang, I was watching Hull Kingston Rovers on the telly so it must've been a Saturday. It was Dan's wife. She'd just found his body in one of the sheds. He'd blown his brains out. He'd taken a length of half inch diameter steel pipe and welded in a spring and bolt assembly. He'd built his own gun. At the funeral I told the story of him stitching the casing of the standing engine. An old farmer come up to me outside, afterwards, and said the standing engine was his, and was still working.

A car is heard pulling up outside.

Shit!

He slightly panics. Stops the cassette. Ejects the tape, puts it in its case and opens the door of the cabinet, which is not locked, and slings the cassette in the cabinet. He puts another tape into the cassette and presses play. The tape is the Jim Reeves song 'Bimbo'.

He fakes that he's asleep. The door opens and in comes **Tina** *with a shopping bag branded Yorkshire Trading Company Ltd.* **Tina** *joins in the song, and bops a little too.*

Enter **Florence** *helped by* **Rob**.

Rob   Now there's the big step in.

Tina   He's having his afternoon nap.

Florence   Is he heckers like. He can't have a nap when Bimbo's blasting out.

Jack (*without moving or opening his eyes*)   I'm ninety-one I'll have a nap whenever I bloody well like!

Tina *gives him the Yorkshire Trading Co. bag. Then sits on the sofa.*

Tina   New pyjamas, Dad.

Jack   What do I need them for?

Florence   You're going into hospital.

Jack   I'm not staying in.

Tina   They advise that you pack a bag, in case they want to keep you in.

Rob   Depending on the MRI, they might need to operate as soon as.

Jack They won't operate on a ninety-one-year-old.

Florence (*serving hatch opens*) They might want to take your prostrate out.

Jack Prostate.

Florence I just said that.

Jack You said prostrate.

Florence I know I did. That's what he's got, an enlarged prostrate!

Jack Prostate!

Florence Why do you keep repeating everything I say! Every time I say prostrate you say prostrate.

Jack Prostate.

Florence Stop doing that!

Jack At my age it's perfectly normal to have an enlarged prostate.

Florence I'm your age, I don't have an enlarged prostrate.

Jack Prostate!

Florence He's doing it again!

Jack You don't have a prostate!

Florence I must have I've never had owt tekken out!

Jack You're a woman!

Florence What's that got to do with it?

Jack Women don't have prostates. It'd be like me complaining about mi buzzwhams.

Florence You don't have buzzwhams!

Jack Exactly! You don't have a prostate.

Florence   You're an expert on women all of a sudden are you?

Jack   Yis!

Florence   I'll put the kettle on. Do you –

Jack   – no!

Rob   Yes please, Mum.

Tina   Please.

Rob   Seeing a GP yesterday, instead of waiting for your own GP, has bought us a week.

Tina   Two weeks. Did you like the doctor, yesterday?

Jack (*showing his middle finger*)   There was a time when an Englishman could expect to die, having lived four score years and ten, without ever having had a stranger shove his finger up his arse.

Tina   Digitial rectal examination.

Rob   Did you like him?

Jack   If he knows as much about cancer as he does about Pakistani cricket we'll be alright.

Rob   He may have saved your life.

Jack   I've had my life, I don't need it saving.

Enter **Florence** *with tray of tea.*

Florence   Lucky I washed your bits before you went in. You're not getting tea.

Jack   Why not?

Florence   You didn't want tea.

Jack   That was before the prostate argument, I've been shouting for ten minutes, mi throat's dry.

Florence   Here, take your pills.

Jack   I've taken mi pills!

Florence   I didn't mean take your pills, I meant don't forget to take your pills.

Jack   I'm not going anywhere till Thursday.

Florence   He'll forget these.

Tina *takes a look at the pill tray.*

Tina   Still on warfarin?

Jack   Rat poison. Whatever's wrong with you they give you warfarin. Eczema, broken leg, depression, crabs.

Florence   Are you gonna try on them new pyjamas?

Jack   No one tries on pyjamas!

Florence   I do.

Jack   You try 'em on then!

Florence   They're not for me, they're for you!

Doorbell.

Who's that now?

Jack   Let 'em in and you might find out.

Tina *goes to the door.* **Rob** *looks out the window.*

Rob   It's Pammy.

Tina   It's locked!!! Why???!!!

Jack   Like a bloody vulture round a carcass.

Rob *goes to the door wielding his key. Opens the door.*

Rob   Hi.

Pammy *enters, kicks her shoes off.* **Florence** *heads for the door to lock it.* |

Pamela   Hello!

Tina   Mum, don't lock the door.

Florence *locks the door.*

Florence   She's in now.

Tina   Mum, why have you locked the door?

Jack   You don't want to know.

Pamela   I know.

Rob   You know? And we don't.

Tina   What is there to know?

Jack   Forty year back, when I fost retired and made the terrible mistake of buying a house in this bloody rain trap –

Florence   – it's not called Wetwang for nothing.

Jack   Alf Pickering from number seven saw your mother planting pampas grass out the front.

Tina   Why did you plant pampas grass, Mum?

Florence   I like the tufts.

Jack   She knows nowt about owt.

Rob   What's the thing everyone knows about pampas grass?

Florence   It's a perennial. Likes the sun.

Jack   You might as well have put a sign up saying we'll have sex with anyone and everyone.

Tina   Did something happen? (*To* **Rob**.) Have you heard this one?

Rob   Nope!

Pamela   I know it.

Jack   Alf Pickering –

Florence   – award winning butcher.

Jack   Who's telling this story?!

Florence   You missed out his awards.

Jack   He gives himself them awards. Alf Pickering –

Florence   – his awards don't matter no more.

Tina   Why not?

Florence   'Cause he's dead.

Jack   He died over thirty years ago!

Florence   I never said I was reading the news.

Jack   Alf Pickering, he come down the path –

Florence   – he give me one of them opera ice creams –

Tina   Eh?

Jack (*singing*)   Justa one Cornetto!

Florence   Followed me into the kitchen and then he took it out –

Tina   – took what out?

Florence   His. . . you know, his chopper!

Tina (*gasps*)   Mother?!

Florence   That's what your dad calls it.

Jack   My fault then!

Florence   I'd done nothing to cncourage him.

Jack   You were out there, with nowt on, planting bloody pampas grass!

Tina   Looking like a very attractive fifty-year-old.

Rob   It's a swingers' flag, Mum.

Tina   Wife swapping!

Florence   You didn't stop me!

Jack   Oh, go on, blame me!

Florence   You drove me to the garden centre.

Rob   Good point. Dad?

Jack   I give up. You want my car then do you, Pam?

Pamela   Yeah, I like it. Has it got an MOT?

Jack   I'm a retired police officer, what do you think?

Pamela   What do you want for it?

Jack   Let's talk money.

Florence   Give her it!

Jack   Keep out of this, will yer!

Florence   You've no interest in money. Never bought a lottery ticket in his life.

Jack   We have premium bonds!

Pamela   I think five hundred is fair.

Jack   The tyres cost me two hundred.

Pamela   It's ten years old.

Jack   It's only got eighteen thousand miles on the clock.

Florence   And all of that is Wetwang to Driffield and back.

Jack   What's your point?

Florence   So she knows where it's been.

Jack   It's irrelevant where it's been.

Florence   If you'd been back and forth across the Sahara sixty times –

Jack   – it's not been back and forth across the Sahara sixty times!

Florence   That's what I'm saying. It's mainly Wetwang to Driffield and back.

Rob   Mum's point is a good point, well made.

Jack   Pam, were you aware that my Lexus IS 200 SE with heated fronted seats and leather upholstery, has not been driven sixty times back and forth across the Sahara?

Pamela   That's good to know.

Florence   Give her the car, we don't need it!

Jack   It's worth a thousand pounds.

Pamela   I don't want you to give it to me.

Jack   With a discount for doing our shopping?

Tina   Dad? Please. That's a bit unnecessary.

Pamela   I don't expect a discount.

Jack   Eddie offered me seven hundred.

Tina   We're not having anything to do with Eddie.

Pamela   Have you told the police?

Florence   He doesn't want to get the police involved.

Pamela   For the best.

Florence   He's embarrassed. Aren't you? Eddie's made a fool of you.

Jack   Fool of us. It's a joint account.

Pamela   And he wangled your allotment out of you.

Jack   I give him the allotment!

Pamela *stands.*

Pamela   I can't afford seven hundred.

Florence   You don't need the car. Tina, Rob's taking you to Hull on Monday.

Pamela *makes to leave.*

Pamela   What's in Hull?

Tina   MRI scan. Prostate.

Pamela   Ooh, they're horrible. MRIs. Claustrophobic. And for prostate you'll have to go all the way into the tube. Bye. I can't shop for you next week. Me and Philip, we're going away. Poole. Hotel du Vin.

Tina   Nice.

Pamela   I hope the scan goes well.

She exits. Door closes.

Tina   Who's Philip?

Florence   Her new fancy man.

Tina   Oh yeah. What does Auntie Vicky say about him?

Florence   She's not met him yet.

Rob   He must have a bit of dosh. Hotel du Vin. You've got to pay good money for a bath in the middle of the room.

Jack   But she hasn't got seven hundred for a Lexus.

Tina   You've done Hotel du Vin, have you? Possibly a fit, skinny dark professional person.

Florence   I'll get on with the cooking.

Tina   What are we having tonight, Mum?

Florence   Cauliflower cheese.

Jack   Oh lord! It's not the Second World War no more. Rationing's gone. Fish pie; cauliflower cheese; fried bread; toad in the hole; scrambled bloody egg; shepherd's pie; sausage and mash; kippers. I'd like sirloin steak once a year, please?!

Rob   I love Mum's cauliflower cheese.

Jack   We're bloody loaded. A police pension, twenty thousand pounds in premium bonds, each! And I win every month.

Tina   Do you?

Jack   Fifty or a hundred, yeah.

Florence (*serving hatch opens*)   I never win!

Jack   Start going to church then!

Florence (*serving hatch*)   You don't go to church.

Jack   I don't need to, I'm already winning!

Florence (*serving hatch*)   It's not fair, it's always him who wins.

Jack   Stop it with that hatch!

Rob   I'm getting premium bonds.

Jack   Rob, ask your mum to come in here. I want a word.

Rob *looks at* **Tina** *and leaves for the kitchen.* **Tina** *thinks and then stands and also leaves for the kitchen.* **Florence** *enters.*

Florence   What is it now?

Jack   I want you to wash me.

Florence   Oh no. What's happened? While we was shopping?

Jack   No. When I'm dead. I want you to wash me when I'm dead.

Florence   Of course. I was always going to. I'll not let anyone else touch you. Is that it?

Jack   Aye.

Florence *goes to the hatch, opens it.*

Florence   The coast's clear!

Enter **Rob** *and* **Tina**.

Rob   We've had an idea. Let's eat out. I'll pay.

Tina   We'll pay.

Jack   We can't go out.

Rob   Everywhere has toilets, Dad.

Florence (*serving hatch opens*)   I've cut the cauli up.

Tina   It won't waste. We'll get a table, it's Tuesday. Where do you want to go?

Rob   Bainton.

Jack   I can't go to Bainton.

Tina   Why not?

Jack   I'm not explaining.

Tina   We can go anywhere, Dad.

Tina *is on her smart phone.*

Eat what you want.

Rob   Steak.

Jack   We're too old. We're embarrassing.

Rob   We're proud of you.

Tina   Both of you.

Tina *stands and makes the phone call.*

Florence (*serving hatch opens*)   Get a table near the toilets.

Jack   I don't want to be near the toilets.

Tina   That's a yes.

(*On phone.*) Hi, do you have a table for four please, today? About seven . . . lovely.

Jack   Who's she talking to?

Rob   Bainton. The restaurant.

Jack   Oh dear.

Florence (*serving hatch open*)   Oh no, we can't go to Bainton!

Tina (*on the phone*)   Kirk. Jack and Florence Kirk . . . yes!
The retired copper . . . that's my father . . . Ha, ha. See you
later.

(*Off the phone.*) He says he knows you.

Jack   I should think he does. I locked him up for ten years.

End of scene.

Epilogue

A year later. There are five large garden waste bags open on the floor. One is full of framed photographs; a second has small electrical items; a third is men's clothes; the fourth is women's clothes; a fifth is full of rubbish/landfill. Pictures have been taken down off the walls, so they leave the tell-tale mark of where they've been. A mirror remains on the wall. The sofa and two big armchairs are gone. The cabinet is still there, but open. A Crock-Pot, Breville and toaster are on the serving hatch shelf waiting to be processed. **Tina** *is on a Zoom call with a female colleague using her laptop hot spotted by her iPhone. She wears a Covid mask, as does the employee.*

Tina   Don't send contracts to Melbourne until Dipak has had his say.

Colleague   Cool.

Tina   Good. I'm signing off.

Colleague   Enjoy the skip.

Tina   I absolutely adore a recycling centre. Bye!

Tina *clicks out.* **Rob** *enters down the stair lift with a handful of men's clothes.*

Rob (*from the stair lift*)   Do you want the stair lift?

Tina   Fuck off.

Rob *deposits the armful of clothes into the men's bag.* **Tina** *assembles a new cardboard box and starts loading it with books.*

Rob   Why are you wearing a mask on a Zoom?

Tina   I'm setting an example to my staff.

Rob   Do I need to wear a mask, around you?

Tina   No. You're my gang, posse, crew.

Rob   Mum caught Covid off dad. He was her crew.

Tina   Apparently, the paramedic told her not to kiss him.

Rob   I was kinda shocked they still kissed.

Tina   Maybe she loved him.

Rob   Have we decided how Dad caught it?

Tina   He never went out.

Rob   Prostate tests. Nosocomial. Got to be.

Tina   'Nosowhat'?

Rob   Hospital acquired. Nosocomial.

Tina   How is it possible to love someone after seventy years of marriage lockdown?

Rob   It's the kind of love that is never represented in film, TV or gaming.

Tina   Gaming?

Rob   Bigger than film.

He picks up a toaster.

Toaster?

Tina   No. Small appliance recycling.

Rob *places the toaster in the correct bag.*

Rob   Do you think they bought a house in Wetwang because it has the most brilliant recycling centre in Yorkshire?

Tina   Why is it called Wetwang?

Rob   Viking. Wetwang, wet field. Driffield, dry field.

He collects the Crock-Pot.

Tina   Was it just a show? For us. The fighting?

Rob   When no one was around –

Tina   – they were affectionate, loving?

Rob *has the Crock-Pot in hand.*

Rob   No. That would require an agreed plan. Crock-Pot?

Tina   Auntie Vicky doesn't want it, but –

Rob   – Pammy might.

Tina   Pammy's not answering her phone.

Rob *puts the Crock-Pot on the floor downstage right next to a casserole dish and a tagine. He picks up the Breville.*

Rob   Breville?

Tina   No.

Rob   Pammy?

Tina   Aunty Vicky said Pammy wants the Crock-Pot, the casserole. She doesn't want the tagine. Nothing else. Draw a line.

Rob *puts the Breville in the electricals bag.* **Rob** *turns his attention to the cabinet. He takes out the cassette recorder.*

Rob   Nineteen seventy-fiveish Sanyo cassette recorder?

Tina *just looks at him. He puts the cassette player into the electricals bag. He picks up a small pot of things.*

Rob   Nail clippers?

Tina   No thank you.

Rob   I'll have them.

He throws it into an open cardboard box, his stuff.

Pencil sharpener?

He throws it into an open cardboard box, his stuff.

Tina   Oi! You didn't give me a chance.

Rob   You godda be quick. Letter opener?

Tina   No.

Rob *deposits it into the discard box. He pulls out the large tray of tapes.*

Rob   Jim Reeves cassettes. Home taped. Numbered one to twenty-eight.

Tina   Landfill! Please!

Rob *dumps them in the landfill bag.*

Tina   Urgh, I hate Jim Reeves!

Rob   Bimbo, Bimbo –

Tina   – shut up!

Rob   Is your car full?

Tina   You could get the landfill bag in.

Tina *continues with the books.* **Rob** *picks up the landfill bag and exits.* **Tina** *continues with the books.* **Rob** *enters.*

Rob   Tina? You've got ten minutes.

Tina   Before what?

Rob   The skip closes at two!

Tina   Did I know that?

Rob   Don't panic, it's only one minute round the corner. That gives you nine minutes to throw a bag in a skip. Do you want any of these books?

Tina   No!

Tina *is gone.* **Rob** *opens a new garden waste bag for landfill items. From the cabinet he picks up a mouth organ. He blows on it. Puts it in the landfill bag, changes his mind and puts it next to* **Pamela**'s *'maybe' pile. A pack of cards. He throws that into his box. Dominoes; into his box. A police whistle. He blows it. His box. A police truncheon. He taps his head lightly with it.*

Rob   Jesus!

He next finds a clockwork policeman toy. He winds it up and puts it on the glass coffee table. He watches as it dances and waves its truncheon, going round in circles until, inevitably, it falls off the table. Doorbell. **Rob** *goes to the door. Opens it.*

Rob   Ah! Pammy.

Pamela   Hi.

Rob   Come in.

Enter **Pamela** *wearing a full plastic head shield face mask. She starts to slip her shoes off.*

Rob   We've stopped worrying about shoes.

Pamela   My mum said you were starting the clear out.

Rob   Yes. Roll up roll up.

Pamela   What?

Rob   Nothing. We've put the Crock-Pot to one side. There.

Pamela   Thank you.

She goes to pick it up.

Do you want this tagine?

Rob   Take it. The casserole dish, the Crock-Pot and the mouth organ.

Pamela   A mouth organ?

Rob   No?! I thought you might.

Pamela   Why?

Rob   I think of you as . . . Bob Dylan.

He takes the mouth organ and puts it in the landfill bag.

Anything else you've got your eye on?

Pamela   I don't like your tone.

Rob   I'm sorry. Stress! My parents have died!

Pamela   It was lovely. A joint funeral. (*Beat.*) What's happening with the car?

Rob   What were you offering?

Pamela   You want me to buy it?

Rob   I'm sorry, have I got something wrong here?

Pamela   Honestly?

Rob   You offered my father five hundred, I think, when he was alive but now that it's my car, which it isn't, and, of course I'm fucking loaded, you expect it for nothing?

Rob *finds the car keys. He thrusts them into her hands.*

It's yours. Drive it away!

Pamela   The V5C?

Rob   The V5C! Of course!

He roots about amongst a pile of papers on top of the cabinet. He finds a folder with 'Car' written on it.

'Car!' There you go. I expect it'll be in there.

Pamela *finds the V5C and takes it.*

Pamela   I can't drive it today. I'll get Phil to give me a lift over tomorrow. He's only in Pocklington.

Rob   Be nice to meet him.

Pamela *attempts to pick up her things, but can't manage them all.*

Rob   Can you manage? No you can't.

He picks up the tagine. **Pamela** *heads for the door, carrying the Crock-Pot, and casserole dish.*

Rob   I bought them a tagine. Never been out the box. Why did I think that two old Yorkshire folk needed a tagine? But you want it, because you're Hull, which is terribly sophisticated, Philip Larkin, the House Martins, Pauline Prescott, so that's good. It's yours.

Pamela   Has Tina gone home?

Rob   No, if you want to slag her off for leaving Yorkshire when she was eighteen, she'll be back from the skip in a minute.

Pamela   You know what this is, don't you? It's grief.

Rob   I don't think it is grief, I'm pretty sure it's antipathy to you.

Pamela *leaves.* **Rob** *closes the door. He fists the wall.*

Rob   Fuck!

He sinks to the floor with his head in hands for a moment in despair. We hear **Pamela**'s *car start up and move off. He then goes back to the cabinet and comes up with a joke shop rubber prosthetic nose. He puts it on. He looks in a mirror, which is on the wall. He turns away from the mirror and then turns back to it. He takes the mirror off the wall and puts it in the framed pictures bag. The door opens* **Tina** *enters carrying three empty garden bags.* **Rob** *looks at her with the nose on.* **Tina** *laughs.*

Rob   Prosthetic rubber nose?

Tina   Yes please! He used to wear it for tradesmen, plumbers who didn't know him.

Rob   Cyrano de Wetwang.

Tina   Why does the skip have a half day? It's really selfish.

Rob   The lorries come to take the full skips away.

Tina   Ah. Skip people, you are forgiven.

Rob   You want the nose then?

Tina   Yeah. The kids love it.

Rob   Never saw him wear it.

Rob *drops it in* **Tina**'s *box.*

Rob   Did you speak to Pammy?

Tina   I saw her, waited in the street so she could get out the drive but she drove past me without even looking.

Rob   We had a few scratchy words. I gave her dad's car. For free.

Tina   Good. We won't have the hassle of selling it. And she did a lot of 'popping in'.

Rob   Her new fancy man –

Tina   – Phil –

Rob   – will drop her over tomorrow from Pocklington!

Tina   Pocklington?!

Rob   Yes! Oh my God! Fucking Pocklington!

Tina   Shit! No. No. No. He lives in Pocklington?!

Rob   I'm ringing Auntie Vicky. What's her number?

Tina *is ahead of him and already dialing.*

Tina   She's in my contacts.

Rob   Since yesterday.

Tina   Don't you start.

(*On the phone.*) Hello . . . it says on your screen Auntie Vicky . . . it's me, Tina . . . yes, Pammy did pop in . . . er, quick question Auntie Vicky . . .

(*Hand over the phone.*) Why am I asking her where Phil lives?

Rob (*shaking his head*)   Because we could deliver the car.

Tina (*on the phone*)   Do you have Pammy's Philip's address, because we could deliver Dad's car, tomorrow, save them both a trip.

Rob *gives* **Tina** *a pencil and a scrap of paper.*

Tina   Yes, yes, . . . Stanford Avenue, . . . got it . . . yes, thank you Auntie Vicky . . . I've got to be back at work tomorrow but Rob's staying another week. Thanks, bye.

(*Off the phone.*) Fifteen, Stanford Avenue, Pocklington.

Rob   Phil is Rhubarb Fool Ltd.

Tina   Yup!

Rob   What do we do?

Tina   Police. Get him arrested.

Rob   So not only did they steal from Dad –

Tina   – Mum and Dad. Joint account.

Rob   She put the blame on Eddie.

Tina   Planning. Forethought. Malice of. It's so stupid! Why did she think she could get away with it?!

Rob   Dad would say, because she wanted to get caught.

Tina   What does a veterinary nurse earn? She's not going to food banks.

Rob   Is money even the motivation?

Tina   Did you get five hundred pounds from Nanna when you went to university?

Rob   Yes. I spent it on, er . . . whatshername . . . fit, skinny, Jacinta. Jacinta summat.

Tina   Which cousins didn't leave Hull? Andy, Pamela –

Rob   – Tim.

Tina   So if you left for university, remember this, Nanna gave you five hundred pounds and if you stayed in Hull you got nothing.

Rob   Nanna, you fascist! I thought that money was a coming of age thing and everyone got it.

Tina   No! University only. An achievement reward.

Rob   That's ugly.

Tina   Are we definitively saying Pammy is a thief?

Rob (*nodding*)   Venal.

Tina   Oh Jesus. Do we tell anyone? Auntie Vicky?

A car pulls up.

Rob   Is that her come back?

Tina   Rhubarb Eddie.

Rob   Who is now fully exonerated? Is he? Help me!

Doorbell. **Rob** *opens the door.*

Hi Eddie.

Eddie (*off*)   How do?

Rob   Are you coming in?

Eddie (*off*)   You serious?

Rob   Take your wellies off.

Eddie *comes in, wellies off.*

Eddie (*to* **Tina**)   How do, Tina?

Tina   Hi.

Eddie   I know I'm not welcome here, just that Jack said I could have his Harry Ramsden's certificate.

Tina   His what?

Rob   It's in this bag.

Tina   What is it?

Rob *digs around in the framed pictures bag and finds the certificate. He gives it to* **Tina**.

Tina (*reading*)   Harry Ramsden's do hereby certify that Jack Kirk on this day, fifth October two thousand and fifteen, did successfully eat the super massive haddock. This amazing feat took place entirely unaided amidst shouts of 'You'll never eat that haddock'. Signed Harry Ramsden.

Eddie   I wor with him that day. There was a moment 'bout half way through when I didn't think he would do it, looked like he was, you know . . . full. But I kept him going.

Tina   You feel as if it is partly your achievement?

Eddie   And I sorted the framing for him in Driff.

Tina *gives it to* **Eddie**.

Tina   It's yours, Eddie.

Eddie   Ta. I won't forget him, or your mother. She made me laugh.

Rob   You made her laugh.

Tina   Thank you.

Eddie   I got mi chair.

Tina   What?

Eddie   The chair wot was there, the one I sat in for his stories, Giovanni from the skip rang us yesterday. I'd told him to look out for one for us and then the actual chair itsen, turns up.

Rob   That's OK, Eddie. It's yours.

Eddie   Did you get his tapes, his stories?

Rob   How do you mean? 'Get his stories'?

Eddie   He recorded all his stories on cassette. I bought the cassettes for him but I was the only one who knew.

Rob   Oh no.

Eddie   It was a secret project. That was the fun part for him.

Rob   Oh no, oh no.

Rob *sinks to the ground. And puts his head in his hands.*

Eddie   Kept them locked in here. Labelled as if they was Jim Reeves. One to twennie-eight. The first eight was Jim Reeves but from nine onwards they was his stories. Dying Deposition, The Wedding Dress, Cornish Pasties, The Tug Boat Captain, The Coal Man. All the greatest hits.

Rob   Oh Jesus.

Tina   I threw the Jim Reeves cassettes in the skip fifteen minutes ago.

Eddie   Oh fuck.

Rob   Eddie, would Giovanni –

Eddie   – it's half day, innit. Lorry'll been bi now.

Rob   Shit!

Eddie *makes to leave.*

Tina   Eddie, we think we may have made a mistake.

Eddie   Oh aye?

Rob   Accusing you of stealing from our parents.

Eddie   I never took owt.

Tina   We now think someone else did it.

Eddie   Who?

Rob   Not sure we can say.

Eddie   Pammy.

Rob   Until we know for sure I don't want to name names.

Tina   The police are investigating.

Rob   We'd like to apologise. For accusing you. Based on nothing. Sorry.

Tina   Yes, sorry.

Silence. **Eddie** *thinks.*

Eddie   Alright. Tarra.

Eddie *leaves. The door closes.*

Tina   Shit!

Rob   I'll head down the recycling. Are you coming?

Tina   What? To crawl around in a skip looking for cassettes?

Rob   Exactly that, yes! Come on!

Tina   He said the lorry's been.

Rob   How does he know?

The door opens, **Eddie** *comes in. He is carrying the tray of cassettes.*

Eddie   Here you go.

He hands over the tray of cassettes.

Tina   You rescued them?

Eddie   Giovanni rang us. I'd told him to look out for 'em. I was gonna torture you with it. Revenge. But you apologised. Jack told us he wanted his grandkids to have them. The player's gonna be in here, yeah?

He finds the cassette in the electricals bag. And plugs it in.

Any requests?

Rob   Cornish Pasties.

Eddie   A goodie! Early one an' all. Nine or ten.

He takes out a cassette and takes out the sleeve and turns it around.

He wrote the proper titles on the inside sleeve, so if you want the collection sorted, turn all the sleeves inside out. Cornish Pasties. Here you go.

Eddie *puts the cassette in the player and presses play, adjusts the volume. He sits on a box, as do* **Rob** *and* **Tina***.*

Jack (*on tape*)   Number nine, the Cornish Pasties. It was a bitter cold winter night and I was on mi Holderness Road beat on mi tod. On nights the fish and chip shops would give you any left overs they had before they closed. But this was a Monday and in them days chip shops weren't open Mondays.

He walks on down stage right in hospital pyjamas and addresses the audience.

Mackman's bakery was open all night and they gave me two piping hot Cornish pasties. I ate one and I wrapped the other in me hanky and put it under mi helmet, to keep mi head warm.

Eddie *laughs.*

Jack (*on tape*)   I was only twenty yards down the road when I saw the Superintendent pull up in his Jaguar, very unusual. He wound his window down and told me to get in. Now when a beat copper gets into a police car you take your helmet off but I had a Cornish pasty under mine so I kept my helmet on, secured it with one hand, and climbed into the passenger seat with an elaborate swooping bow.

He does the swooping bow.

I secured the helmet by pressing it on to the interior roof of the Jag. The Super give us a funny look but didn't say owt. Residents had complained of screams coming from a scrap yard. Once at the yard the Super jumped out, and watched us as I exited the Jag with the same elaborate swooping manoeuvre, only in reverse.

He performs.

We had to climb the gate into the scrap yard. This I managed to do, whilst keeping one hand on my helmet. The Super watched and frowned again. We quickly found a young man trapped under a van. He had been trying to steal the van's silencer when the jack slipped and the van crushed his legs. I found another jack, set it under the van and the Super started winding it. The lad had been trapped for twelve hours and was starving. I asked him if he fancied a Cornish pastie. The Super stopped winding the jack and looked at me as I lifted up my helmet, took out the Cornish pastie and give it to the lad. The Super said 'Kirk, a Cornish pastie?' I said 'He's unlucky, it's a Monday, any other day of the week he'd be getting haddock and chips and mushy peas'.

Eddie *laughs.* **Rob** *laughs.* **Tina** *is crying.* **Jack** *exits.*

Jack (*on tape*)   He didn't go to prison, but he did lose both his legs. I used to see him in his wheelchair down Holderness Road and he'd always bool over and shake my hand and tell everyone that I saved his life. I didn't save his life, I give him a Cornish pastie and nicked him for tryna steal a silencer.

Eddie *is emotional, head in hands.* **Rob** *stands, and turns the cassette off.*

Rob   Thanks Eddie.

To black.

The end.